SELINA'S **BIG** SCORE

S0-ACV-967

story and art
DARWYN COOKE

color
MATT HOLLINGSWORTH

for candis

3 1558 00209 7491

CATWOMAN: SELINA'S BIG SCORE.
Published by DC Comics,
1700 Broadway, New York, NY 10019.
Copyright © 2002 DC Comics.
All Rights Reserved.
All characters featured in this issue,
the distinctive likenesses thereof,
and all related indicia are
trademarks of DC Comics.
The stories, characters and incidents
mentioned in this magazine
are entirely fictional.
DC Comics does not read
or accept unsolicited submissions
of ideas, stories or artwork.
Printed in Canada.
DC Comics. A division of Warner Bros.-
An AOL Time Warner Company
Cover painting by Darwyn Cooke
HC ISBN 1-56389-897-7   SC ISBN 1-56389-922-1

DC COMICS
Jenette Kahn, President & Editor-in-Chief
Paul Levitz, Executive Vice President & Publisher
Mike Carlin, VP-Executive Editor
Mark Chiarello, Editor
Valerie D'Orazio, Assistant Editor
Amie Brockway-Metcalf, Art Director
Georg Brewer, VP-Design & Retail Product Development
Richard Bruning, VP-Creative Director
Patrick Caldon, Senior VP-Finance & Operations
Terri Cunningham, VP-Managing Editor
Dan DiDio, VP-Editorial
Joel Ehrlich, Senior VP-Advertising & Promotions
Alison Gill, VP-Manufacturing
Lillian Laserson, VP & General Counsel
Jim Lee, Editorial Director-WildStorm
David McKillips, VP-Advertising
John Nee, VP-Business Development
Cheryl Rubin, VP-Licensing & Merchandising
Bob Wayne, VP-Sales & Marketing

morocco

I suppose I should start with the fact that I'm dead.

At least I was declared legally dead, but that's another story.

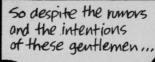

So despite the rumors and the intentions of these gentlemen...

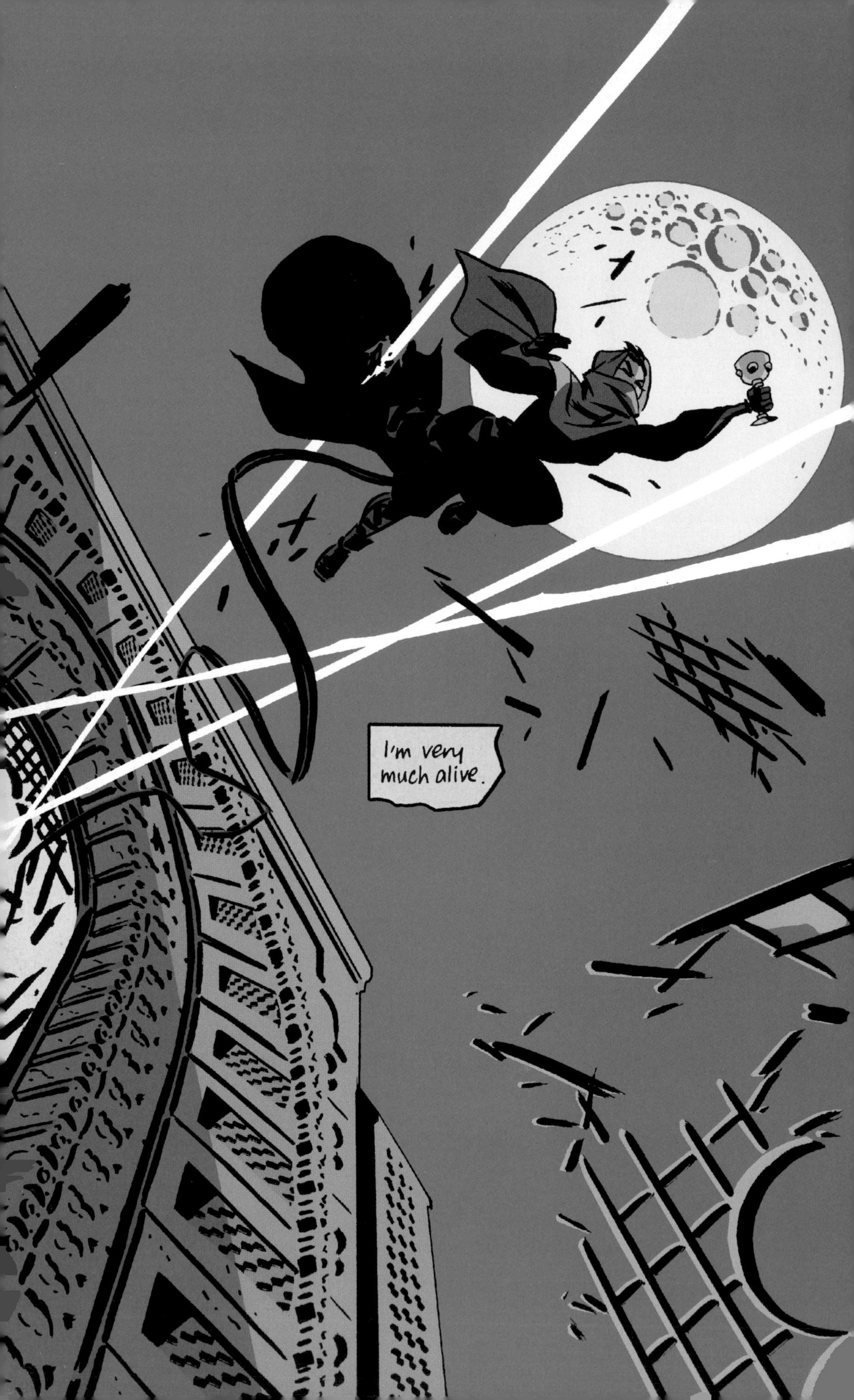
I'm very much alive.

BOOK ONE

SELINA

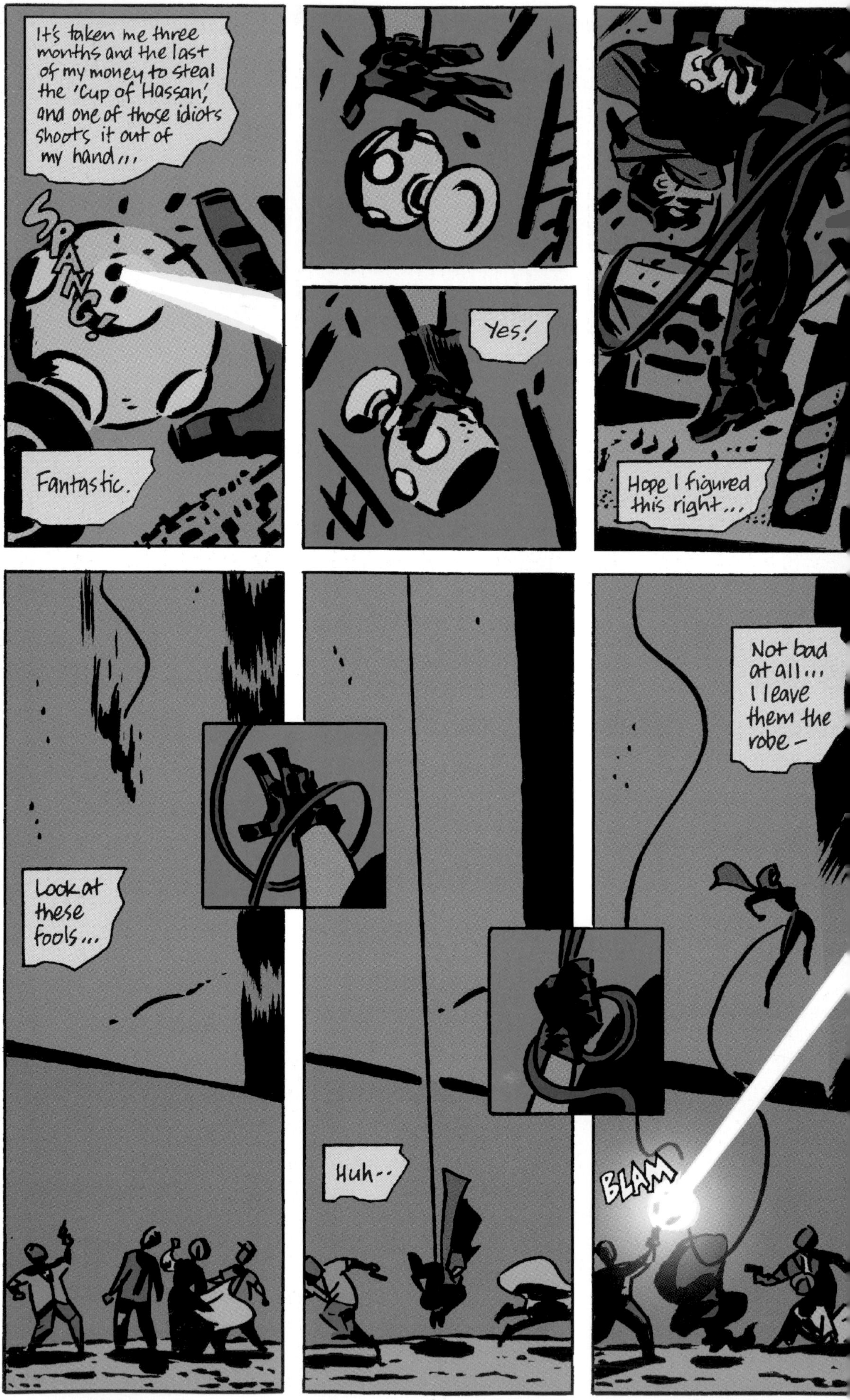
It's taken me three months and the last of my money to steal the 'Cup of Hassan,' and one of those idiots shoots it out of my hand...
SPANG!
Fantastic.
Yes!
Hope I figured this right...
Look at these fools...
Huh..
Not bad at all... I leave them the robe -
BLAM

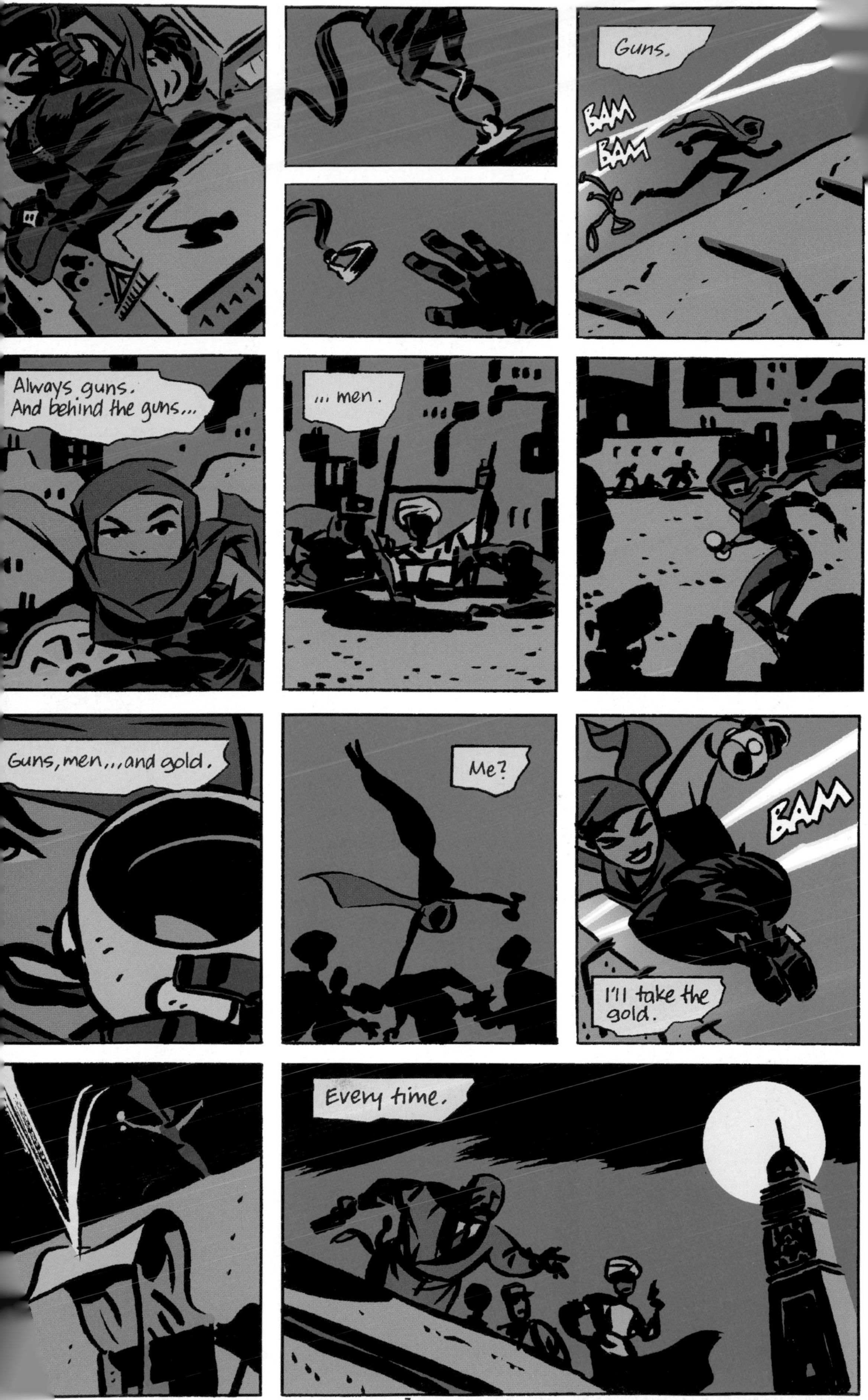
Guns.
BAM
BAM
Always guns.
And behind the guns...
... men.
Guns, men... and gold.
Me?
BAM
I'll take the gold.
Every time.

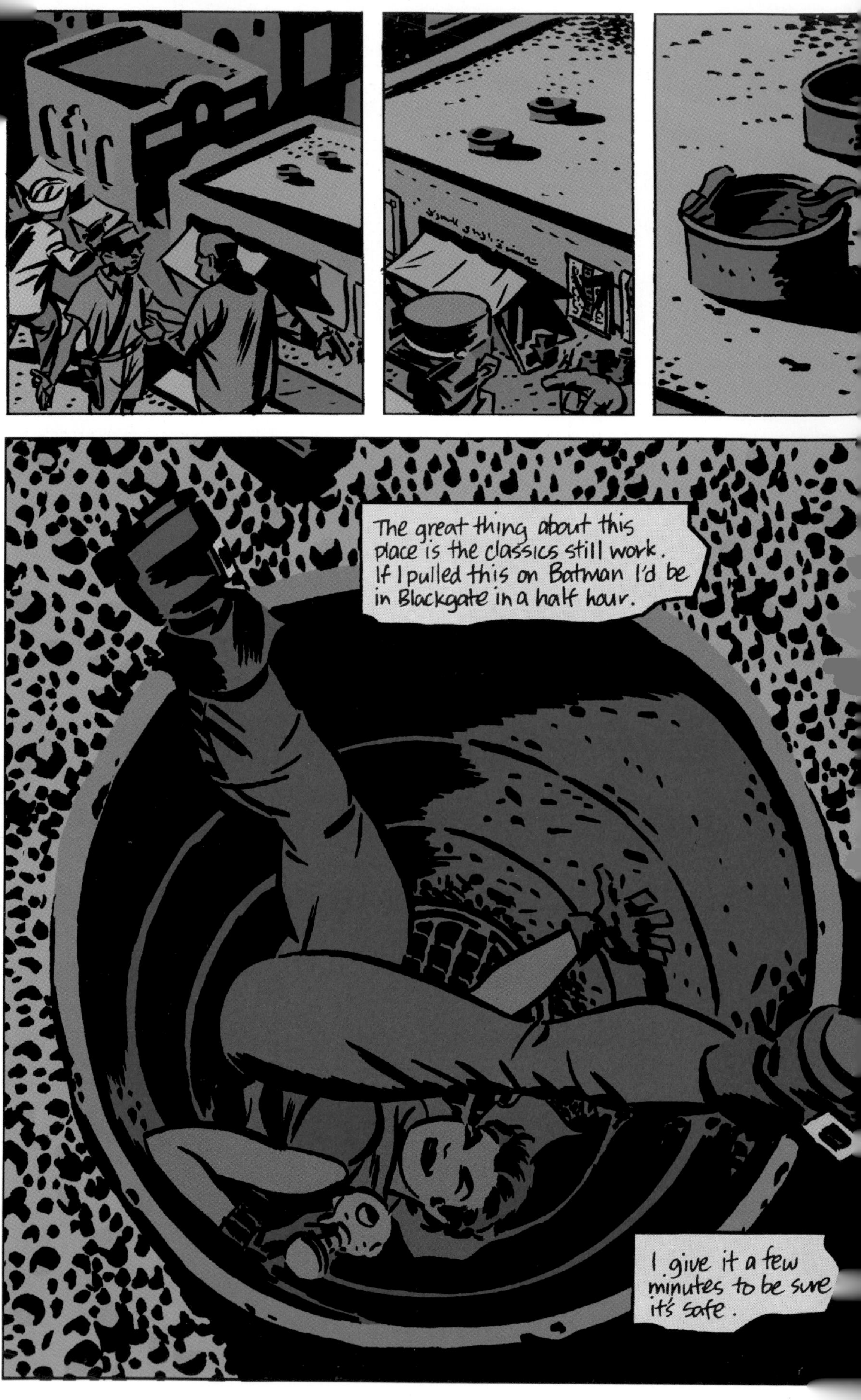
The great thing about this place is the classics still work. If I pulled this on Batman I'd be in Blackgate in a half hour.
I give it a few minutes to be sure it's safe.

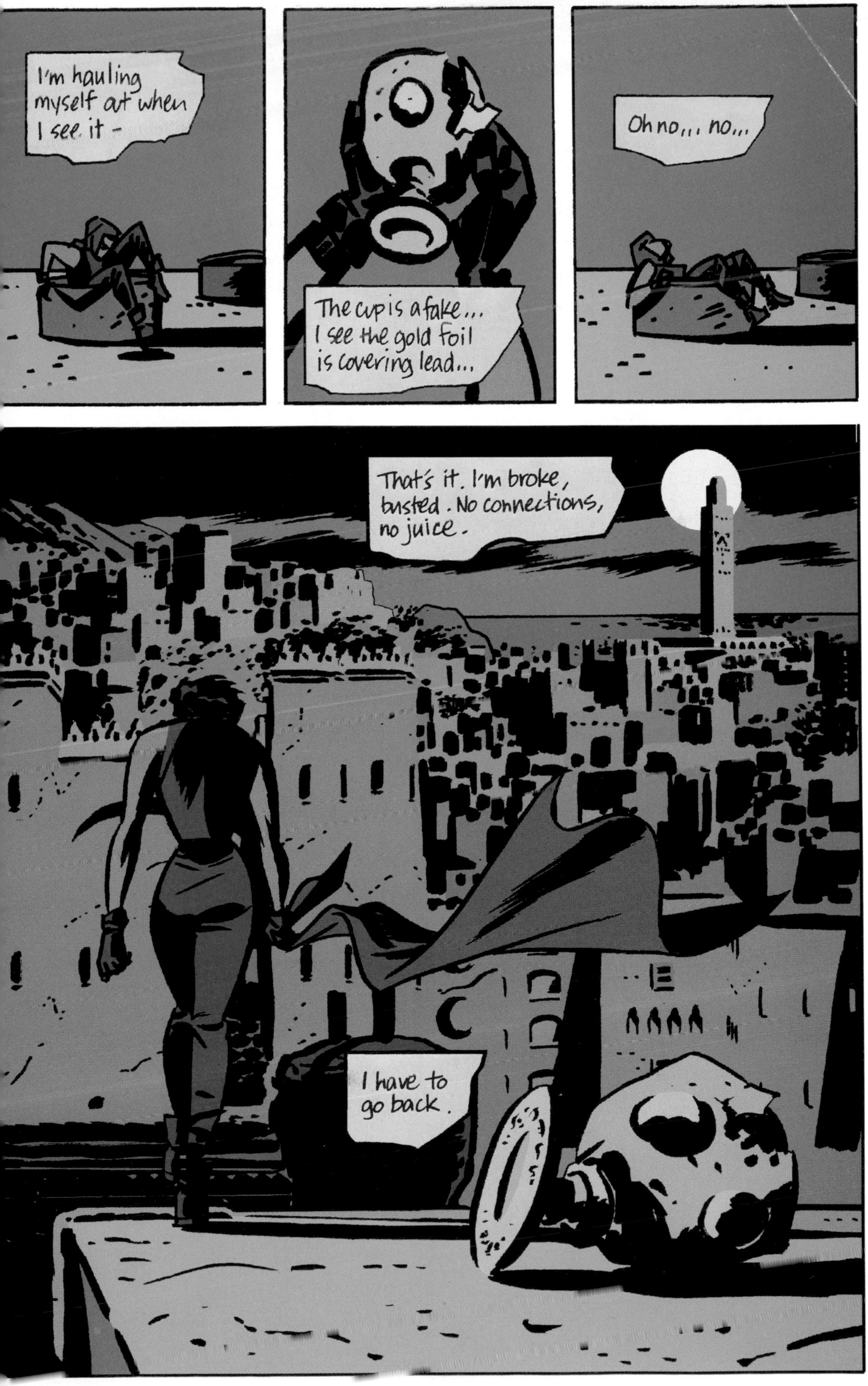
I'm hauling myself out when I see it -
The cup is a fake... I see the gold foil is covering lead...
Oh no... no...
That's it. I'm broke, busted. No connections, no juice.
I have to go back.

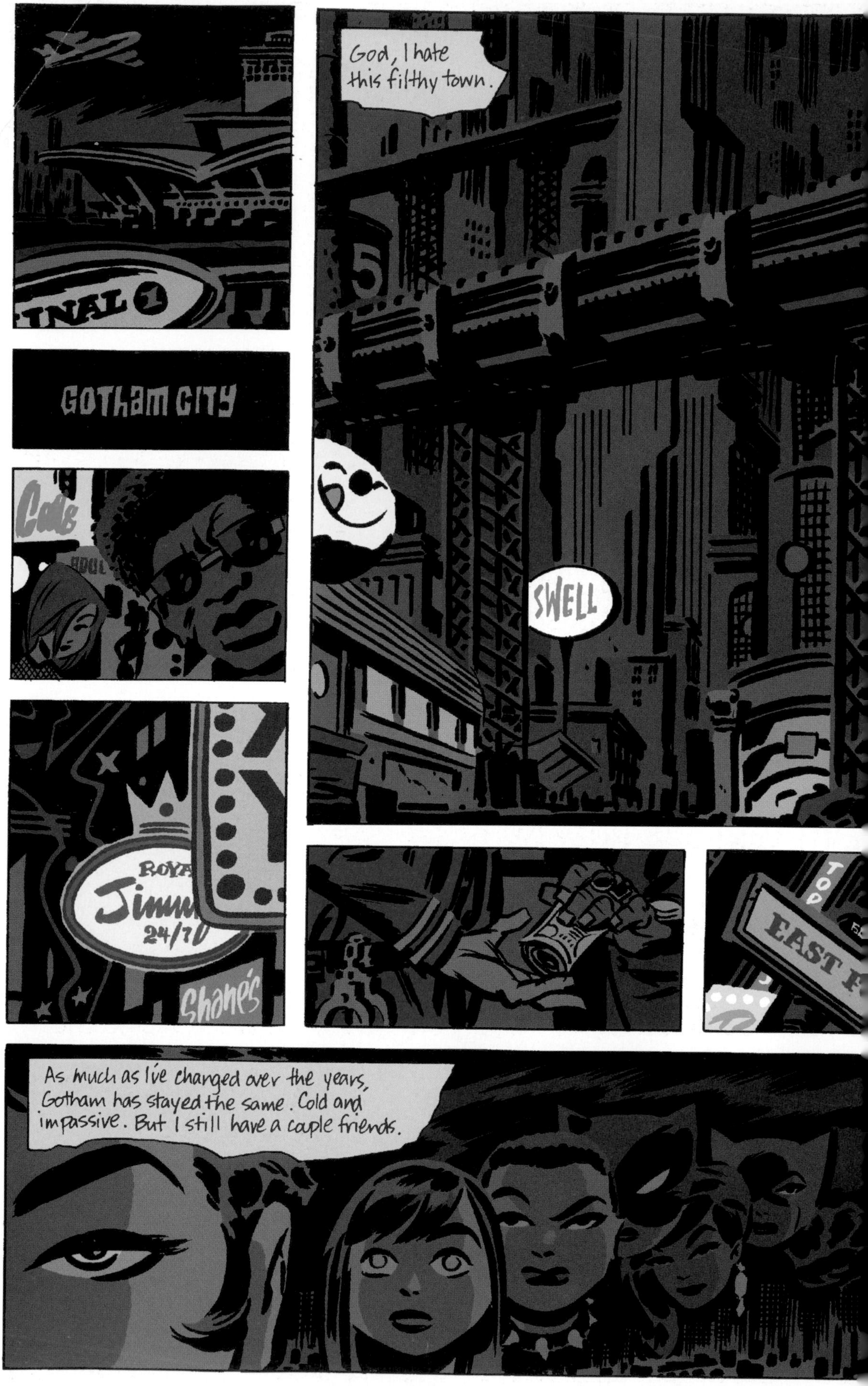
INAL 1
GOTHAM CITY
God, I hate this filthy town.
SWELL
ROYA
Jimm
24/7
Shane's
EAST F
As much as I've changed over the years, Gotham has stayed the same. Cold and impassive. But I still have a couple friends.

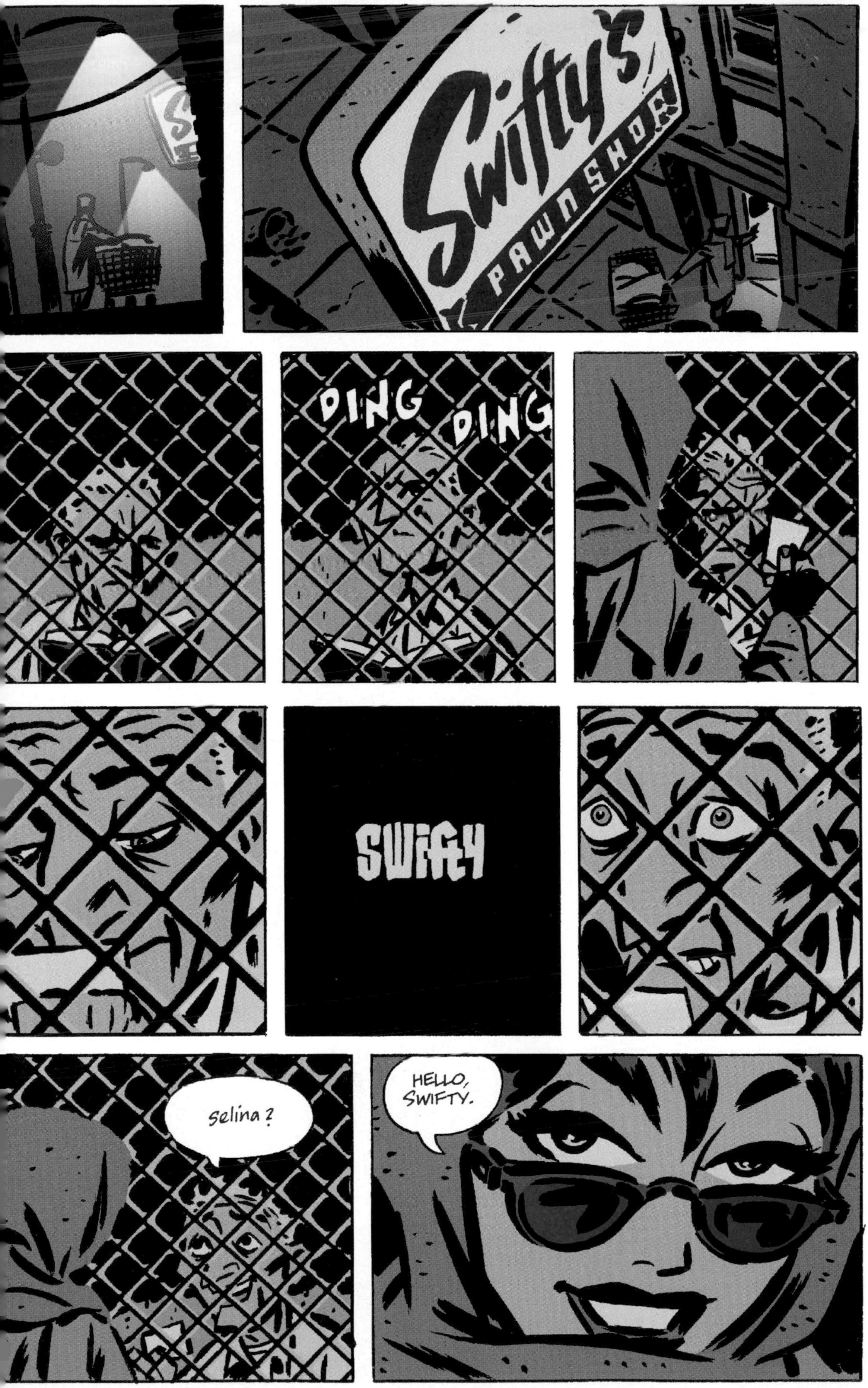
Swifty's
PAWN SHOP
DING DING
SWIFTY
selina?
HELLO, SWIFTY.

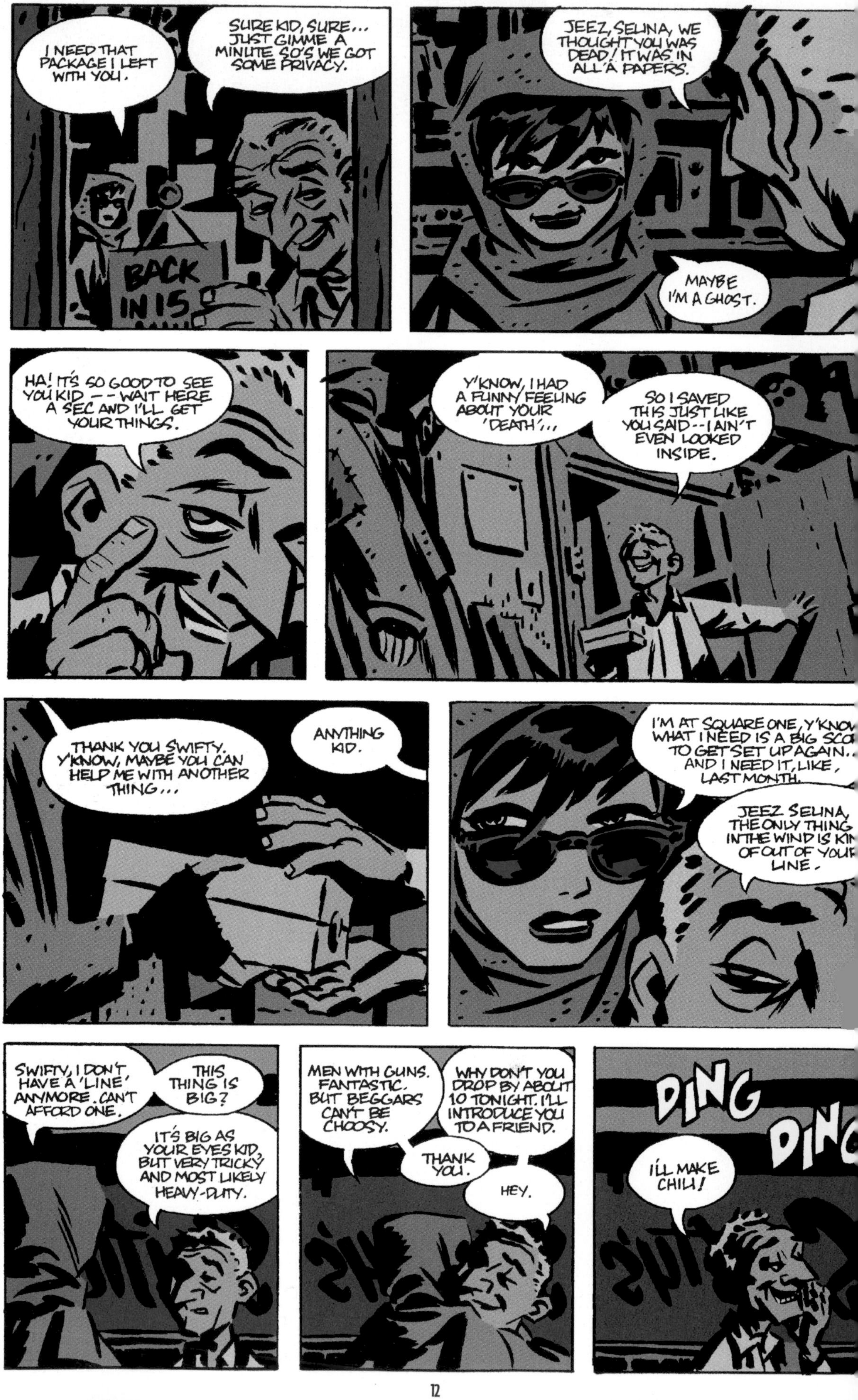
I NEED THAT PACKAGE I LEFT WITH YOU.
SURE KID, SURE... JUST GIMME A MINUTE SO'S WE GOT SOME PRIVACY.
BACK IN 15
JEEZ, SELINA, WE THOUGHT YOU WAS DEAD! IT WAS IN ALL A PAPERS.
MAYBE I'M A GHOST.
HA! IT'S SO GOOD TO SEE YOU KID -- WAIT HERE A SEC AND I'LL GET YOUR THINGS.
Y'KNOW, I HAD A FUNNY FEELING ABOUT YOUR 'DEATH'...
SO I SAVED THIS JUST LIKE YOU SAID--I AIN'T EVEN LOOKED INSIDE.
THANK YOU SWIFTY. Y'KNOW, MAYBE YOU CAN HELP ME WITH ANOTHER THING...
ANYTHING KID.
I'M AT SQUARE ONE, Y'KNOW WHAT I NEED IS A BIG SCO TO GET SET UP AGAIN... AND I NEED IT, LIKE, LAST MONTH.
JEEZ SELINA, THE ONLY THING IN THE WIND IS KIN OF OUT OF YOUR LINE.
SWIFTY, I DON'T HAVE A 'LINE' ANYMORE. CAN'T AFFORD ONE.
THIS THING IS BIG?
IT'S BIG AS YOUR EYES KID, BUT VERY TRICKY AND MOST LIKELY HEAVY-DUTY.
MEN WITH GUNS. FANTASTIC. BUT BEGGARS CAN'T BE CHOOSY.
WHY DON'T YOU DROP BY ABOUT 10 TONIGHT. I'LL INTRODUCE YOU TO A FRIEND.
THANK YOU.
HEY.
DING
DING
I'LL MAKE CHILI!

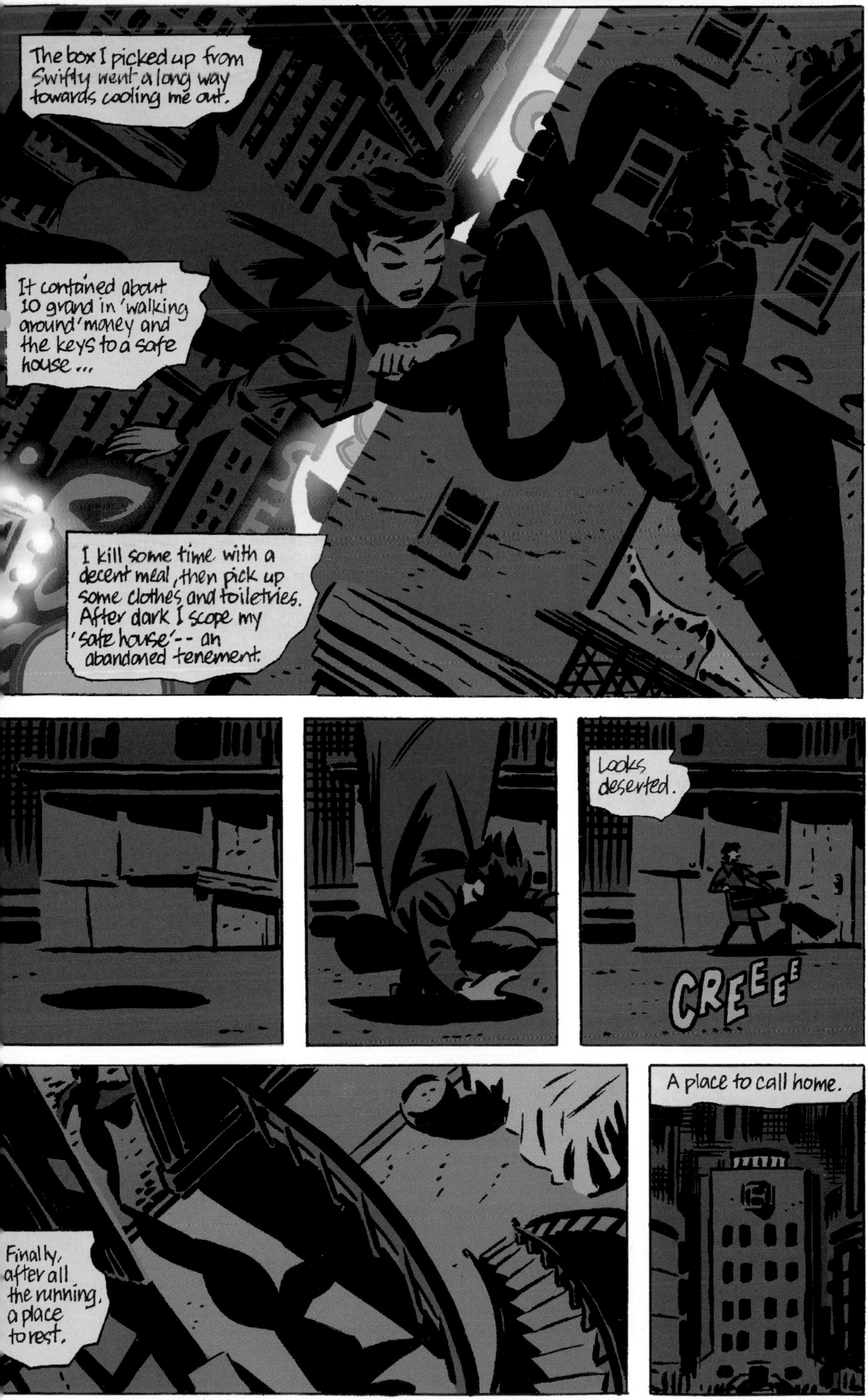
The box I picked up from Swifty went a long way towards cooling me out.
It contained about 10 grand in 'walking around' money and the keys to a safe house...
I kill some time with a decent meal, then pick up some clothes and toiletries. After dark I scope my 'safe house'-- an abandoned tenement.
Looks deserted.
CREEEE
Finally, after all the running, a place to rest.
A place to call home.

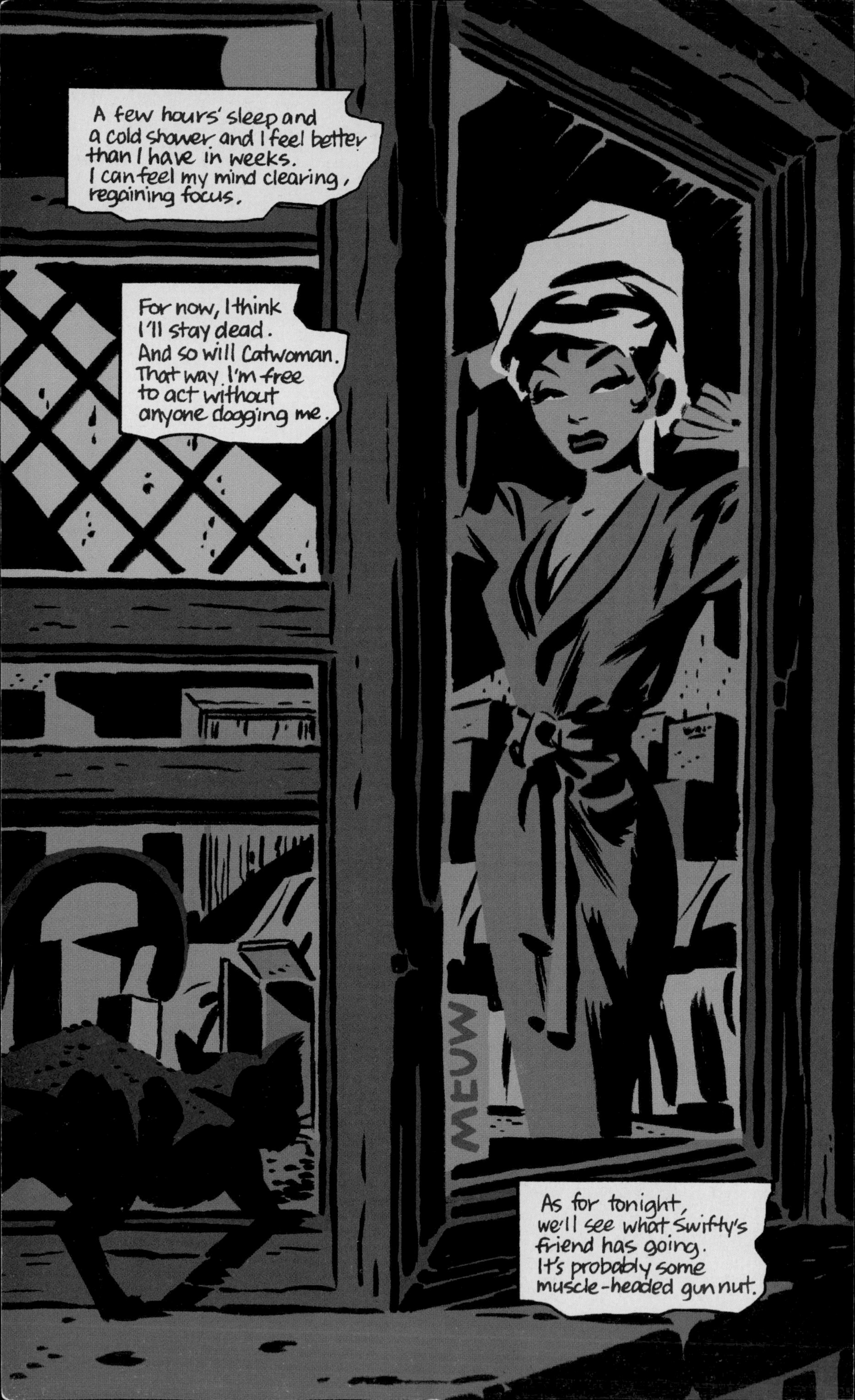
A few hours' sleep and a cold shower, and I feel better than I have in weeks. I can feel my mind clearing, regaining focus.
For now, I think I'll stay dead. And so will Catwoman. That way, I'm free to act without anyone dogging me.
MEUW
As for tonight, we'll see what Swifty's friend has going. It's probably some muscle-headed gun nut.

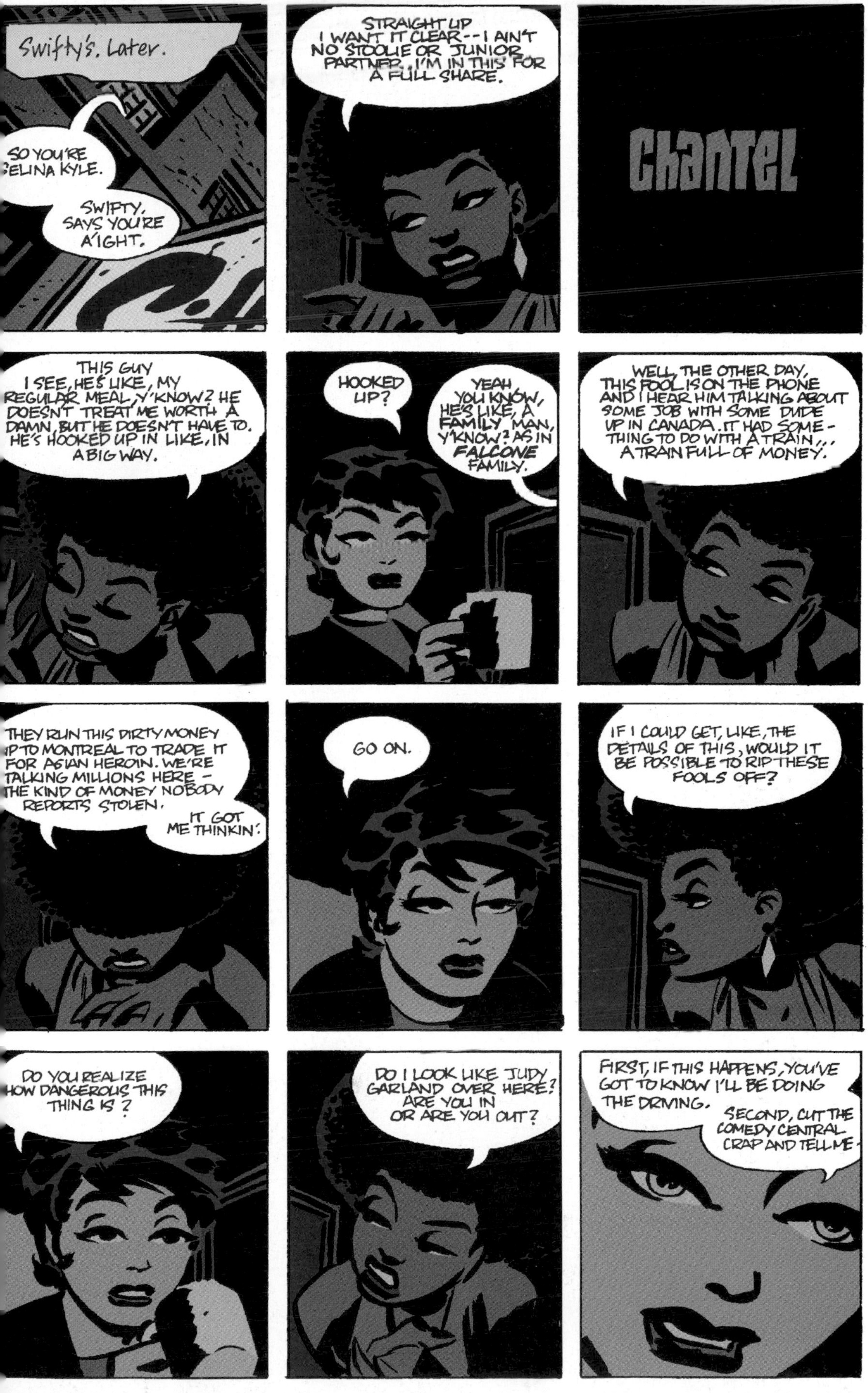
Swifty's. Later.
SO YOU'RE SELINA KYLE.
SWIFTY SAYS YOU'RE A'IGHT.
STRAIGHT UP I WANT IT CLEAR-- I AIN'T NO STOOLIE OR JUNIOR PARTNER. I'M IN THIS FOR A FULL SHARE.
Chantel
THIS GUY I SEE, HE'S LIKE, MY REGULAR MEAL, Y'KNOW? HE DOESN'T TREAT ME WORTH A DAMN, BUT HE DOESN'T HAVE TO. HE'S HOOKED UP IN LIKE, IN A BIG WAY.
HOOKED UP?
YEAH YOU KNOW, HE'S LIKE, A FAMILY MAN, Y'KNOW? AS IN FALCONE FAMILY.
WELL, THE OTHER DAY, THIS FOOL IS ON THE PHONE AND I HEAR HIM TALKING ABOUT SOME JOB WITH SOME DUDE UP IN CANADA. IT HAD SOMETHING TO DO WITH A TRAIN... A TRAIN FULL OF MONEY.
THEY RUN THIS DIRTY MONEY UP TO MONTREAL TO TRADE IT FOR ASIAN HEROIN. WE'RE TALKING MILLIONS HERE - THE KIND OF MONEY NOBODY REPORTS STOLEN.
IT GOT ME THINKIN'.
GO ON.
IF I COULD GET, LIKE, THE DETAILS OF THIS, WOULD IT BE POSSIBLE TO RIP THESE FOOLS OFF?
DO YOU REALIZE HOW DANGEROUS THIS THING IS?
DO I LOOK LIKE JUDY GARLAND OVER HERE? ARE YOU IN OR ARE YOU OUT?
FIRST, IF THIS HAPPENS, YOU'VE GOT TO KNOW I'LL BE DOING THE DRIVING.
SECOND, CUT THE COMEDY CENTRAL CRAP AND TELL ME -

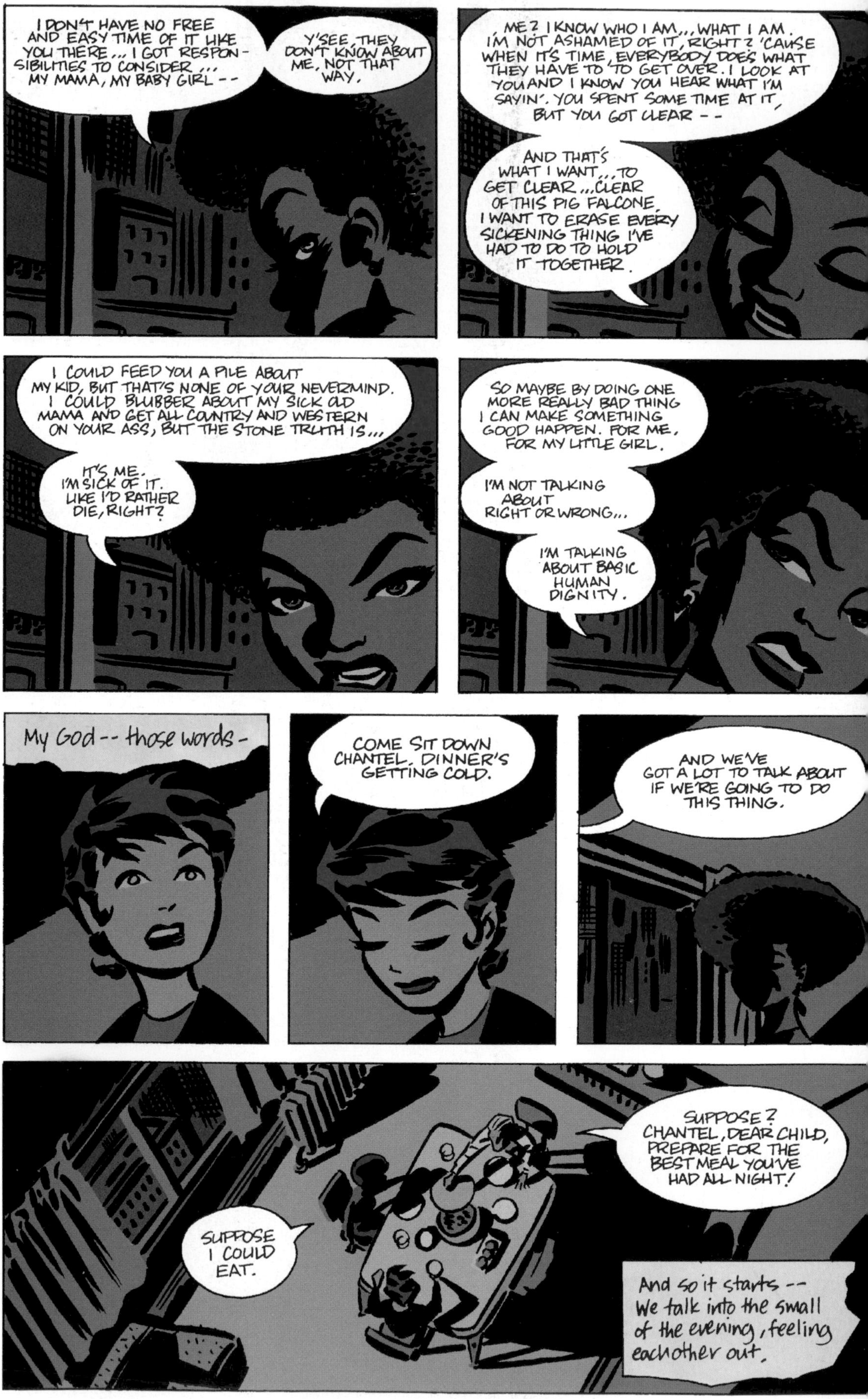

I DON'T HAVE NO FREE AND EASY TIME OF IT LIKE YOU THERE... I GOT RESPONSIBILITIES TO CONSIDER... MY MAMA, MY BABY GIRL --
Y'SEE, THEY DON'T KNOW ABOUT ME, NOT THAT WAY.
ME? I KNOW WHO I AM... WHAT I AM. I'M NOT ASHAMED OF IT, RIGHT? 'CAUSE WHEN IT'S TIME, EVERYBODY DOES WHAT THEY HAVE TO TO GET OVER. I LOOK AT YOU AND I KNOW YOU HEAR WHAT I'M SAYIN'. YOU SPENT SOME TIME AT IT, BUT YOU GOT CLEAR --
AND THAT'S WHAT I WANT... TO GET CLEAR... CLEAR OF THIS PIG FALCONE. I WANT TO ERASE EVERY SICKENING THING I'VE HAD TO DO TO HOLD IT TOGETHER.
I COULD FEED YOU A PILE ABOUT MY KID, BUT THAT'S NONE OF YOUR NEVERMIND. I COULD BLUBBER ABOUT MY SICK OLD MAMA AND GET ALL COUNTRY AND WESTERN ON YOUR ASS, BUT THE STONE TRUTH IS...
IT'S ME. I'M SICK OF IT. LIKE I'D RATHER DIE, RIGHT?
SO MAYBE BY DOING ONE MORE REALLY BAD THING I CAN MAKE SOMETHING GOOD HAPPEN. FOR ME. FOR MY LITTLE GIRL.
I'M NOT TALKING ABOUT RIGHT OR WRONG...
I'M TALKING ABOUT BASIC HUMAN DIGNITY.
My God -- those words -
COME SIT DOWN CHANTEL. DINNER'S GETTING COLD.
AND WE'VE GOT A LOT TO TALK ABOUT IF WE'RE GOING TO DO THIS THING.
SUPPOSE? CHANTEL, DEAR CHILD, PREPARE FOR THE BEST MEAL YOU'VE HAD ALL NIGHT!
SUPPOSE I COULD EAT.
And so it starts -- We talk into the small of the evening, feeling eachother out.

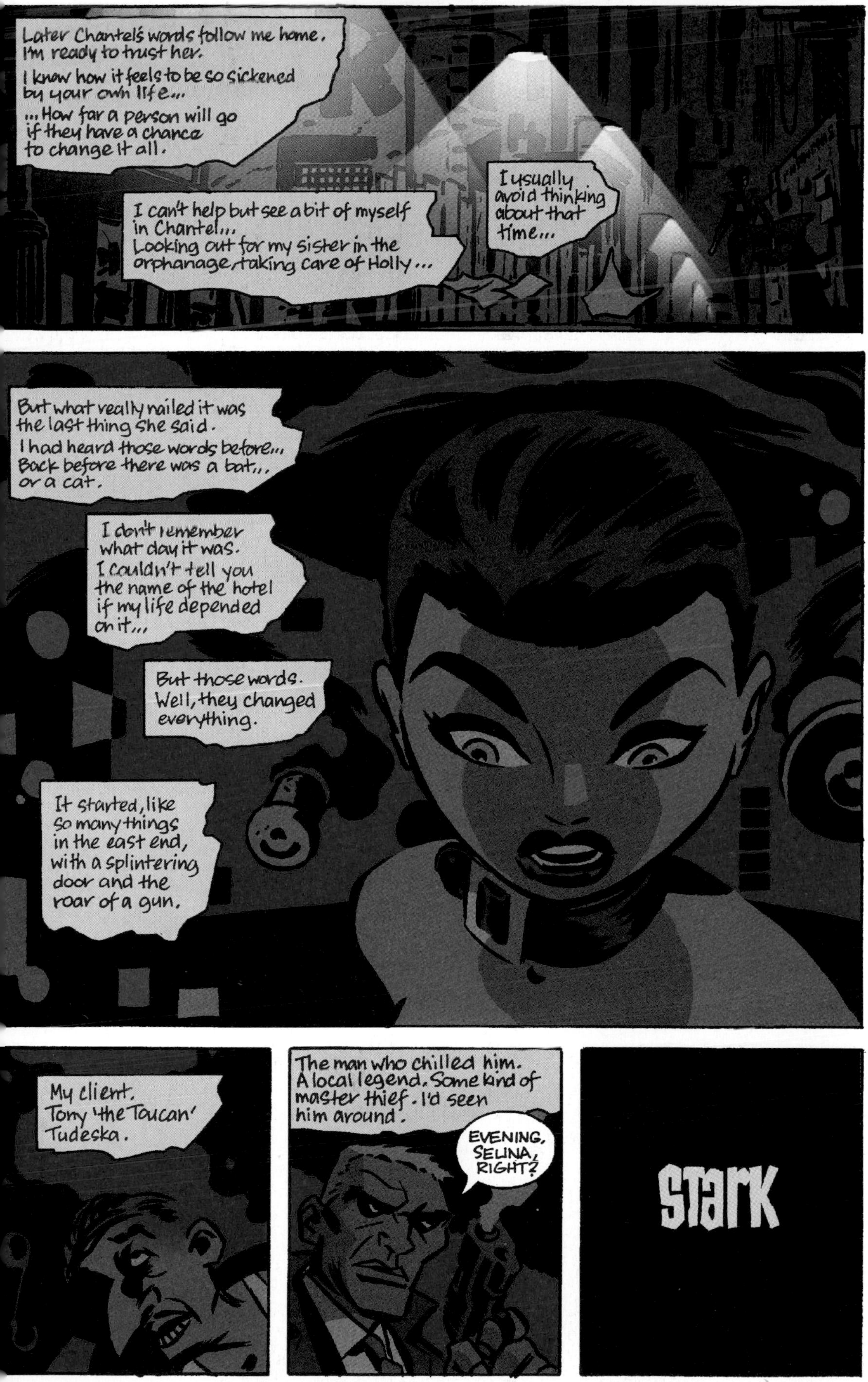
Later Chantel's words follow me home. I'm ready to trust her.
I know how it feels to be so sickened by your own life...
...How far a person will go if they have a chance to change it all.
I can't help but see a bit of myself in Chantel... Looking out for my sister in the orphanage, taking care of Holly...
I usually avoid thinking about that time...
But what really nailed it was the last thing she said.
I had heard those words before... Back before there was a bat... or a cat.
I don't remember what day it was. I couldn't tell you the name of the hotel if my life depended on it...
But those words. Well, they changed everything.
It started, like so many things in the east end, with a splintering door and the roar of a gun.
My client. Tony 'the Toucan' Tudeska.
The man who chilled him. A local legend. Some kind of master thief. I'd seen him around.
EVENING, SELINA, RIGHT?
STARK

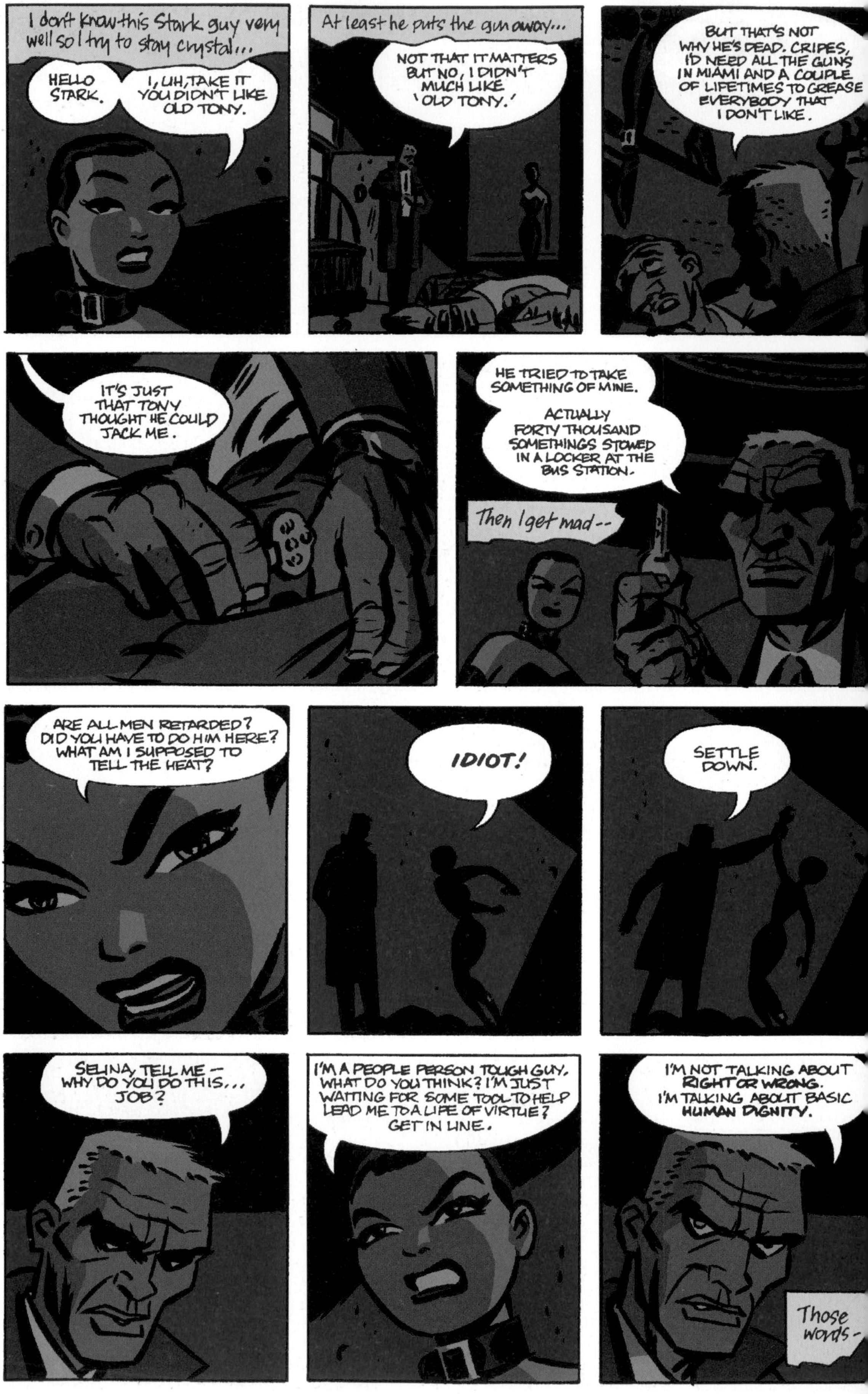
I don't know this Stark guy very well so I try to stay crystal...
HELLO STARK.
I, UH, TAKE IT YOU DIDN'T LIKE OLD TONY.
At least he puts the gun away...
NOT THAT IT MATTERS BUT NO, I DIDN'T MUCH LIKE 'OLD TONY.'
BUT THAT'S NOT WHY HE'S DEAD. CRIPES, I'D NEED ALL THE GUNS IN MIAMI AND A COUPLE OF LIFETIMES TO GREASE EVERYBODY THAT I DON'T LIKE.
IT'S JUST THAT TONY THOUGHT HE COULD JACK ME.
HE TRIED TO TAKE SOMETHING OF MINE.
ACTUALLY FORTY THOUSAND SOMETHINGS STOWED IN A LOCKER AT THE BUS STATION.
Then I get mad--
ARE ALL MEN RETARDED? DID YOU HAVE TO DO HIM HERE? WHAT AM I SUPPOSED TO TELL THE HEAT?
IDIOT!
SETTLE DOWN.
SELINA, TELL ME -- WHY DO YOU DO THIS... JOB?
I'M A PEOPLE PERSON TOUGH GUY, WHAT DO YOU THINK? I'M JUST WAITING FOR SOME TOOL TO HELP LEAD ME TO A LIFE OF VIRTUE? GET IN LINE.
I'M NOT TALKING ABOUT RIGHT OR WRONG. I'M TALKING ABOUT BASIC HUMAN DIGNITY.
Those words-

YOU KNOW YOU'RE BETTER THAN THIS BUT THERE'S NOTHING TO BELIEVE IN. NO ONE TO TRUST.

LET ME GUESS. I COULD TRUST YOU, RIGHT?

HEH. GOOD ONE.

NO.

TRUST YOURSELF. IF YOU'RE GOING TO SPEND YOUR LIFE ON THIS SIDE OF THE LAW, AND YOU WANT TO SURVIVE...

YOU HAVE TO CARE ABOUT YOURSELF. LET ME SHOW YOU.

His touch... as cold and sure as... my own.

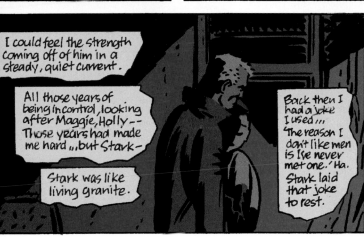

I could feel the strength coming off of him in a steady, quiet current.

All those years of being in control, looking after Maggie, Holly -- Those years had made me hard ...but Stark—

Stark was like living granite.

Back then I had a joke I used ... 'The reason I don't like men is I've never met one.' Ha. Stark laid that joke to rest.

I left with him that night. I could never tell Holly or others about him. It was a world of two.

There were other men who taught me, like Ted Grant.

But none of them were as frankly amoral as Stark.

He promised to teach me, and was good as his word -- Which is more than I can say for myself.

And now here I am with the biggest payoff since Lufthansa and I screwed over the one man who could help me.

In other words, karmic par for my course.

SWIFTY? YES. TELL CHANTEL WE ARE ON. I'LL GET YOU SPECS FOR SOME LISTENING HARDWARE I'LL NEED...

WELL NOW, THAT'S JUST IT. WE NEED A PRO -- SOMEONE WITH THE KNOW-HOW AND THE JUICE TO PULL THIS TOGETHER.

I WANT YOU TO CALL STARK.

SELINA, HAVE YOU LOST YOUR MIND? YOU JUST GOT BACK FROM THE DEAD, FOR PETE'S SAKE!

AFTER WHAT HAPPENED BETWEEN YOU TWO ...

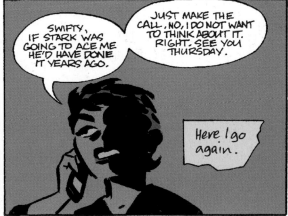

SWIFTY, IF STARK WAS GOING TO ACE ME HE'D HAVE DONE IT YEARS AGO.

JUST MAKE THE CALL. NO, I DO NOT WANT TO THINK ABOUT IT. RIGHT. SEE YOU THURSDAY.

Here I go again.

19

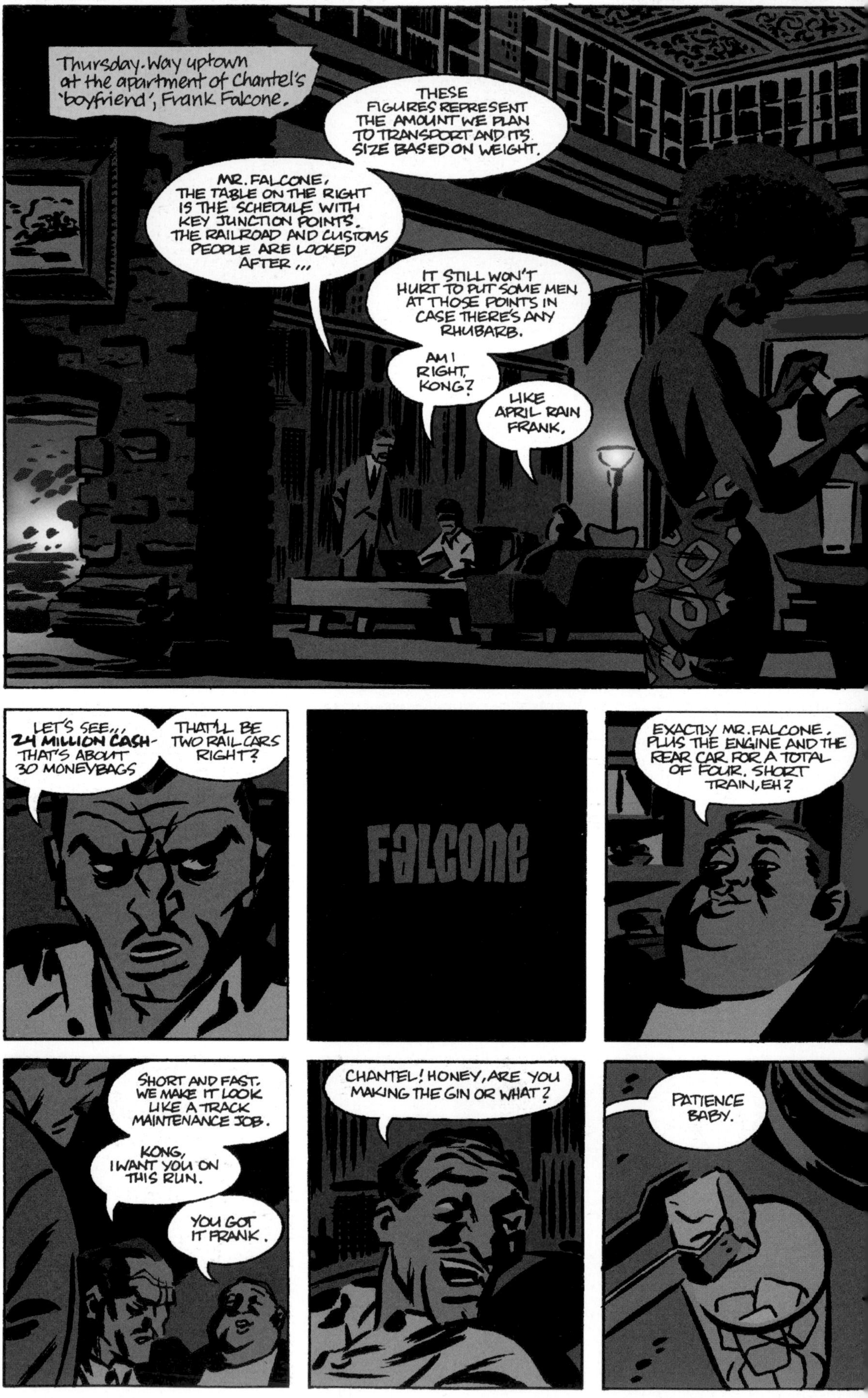
Thursday. Way uptown at the apartment of Chantel's 'boyfriend', Frank Falcone.
THESE FIGURES REPRESENT THE AMOUNT WE PLAN TO TRANSPORT AND ITS SIZE BASED ON WEIGHT.
MR. FALCONE, THE TABLE ON THE RIGHT IS THE SCHEDULE WITH KEY JUNCTION POINTS. THE RAILROAD AND CUSTOMS PEOPLE ARE LOOKED AFTER...
IT STILL WON'T HURT TO PUT SOME MEN AT THOSE POINTS IN CASE THERE'S ANY RHUBARB.
AM I RIGHT, KONG?
LIKE APRIL RAIN FRANK.
LET'S SEE... **24 MILLION CASH**- THAT'S ABOUT 30 MONEYBAGS
THAT'LL BE TWO RAIL CARS RIGHT?
FALCONE
EXACTLY MR. FALCONE. PLUS THE ENGINE AND THE REAR CAR FOR A TOTAL OF FOUR. SHORT TRAIN, EH?
SHORT AND FAST. WE MAKE IT LOOK LIKE A TRACK MAINTENANCE JOB.
KONG, I WANT YOU ON THIS RUN.
YOU GOT IT FRANK.
CHANTEL! HONEY, ARE YOU MAKING THE GIN OR WHAT?
PATIENCE BABY.

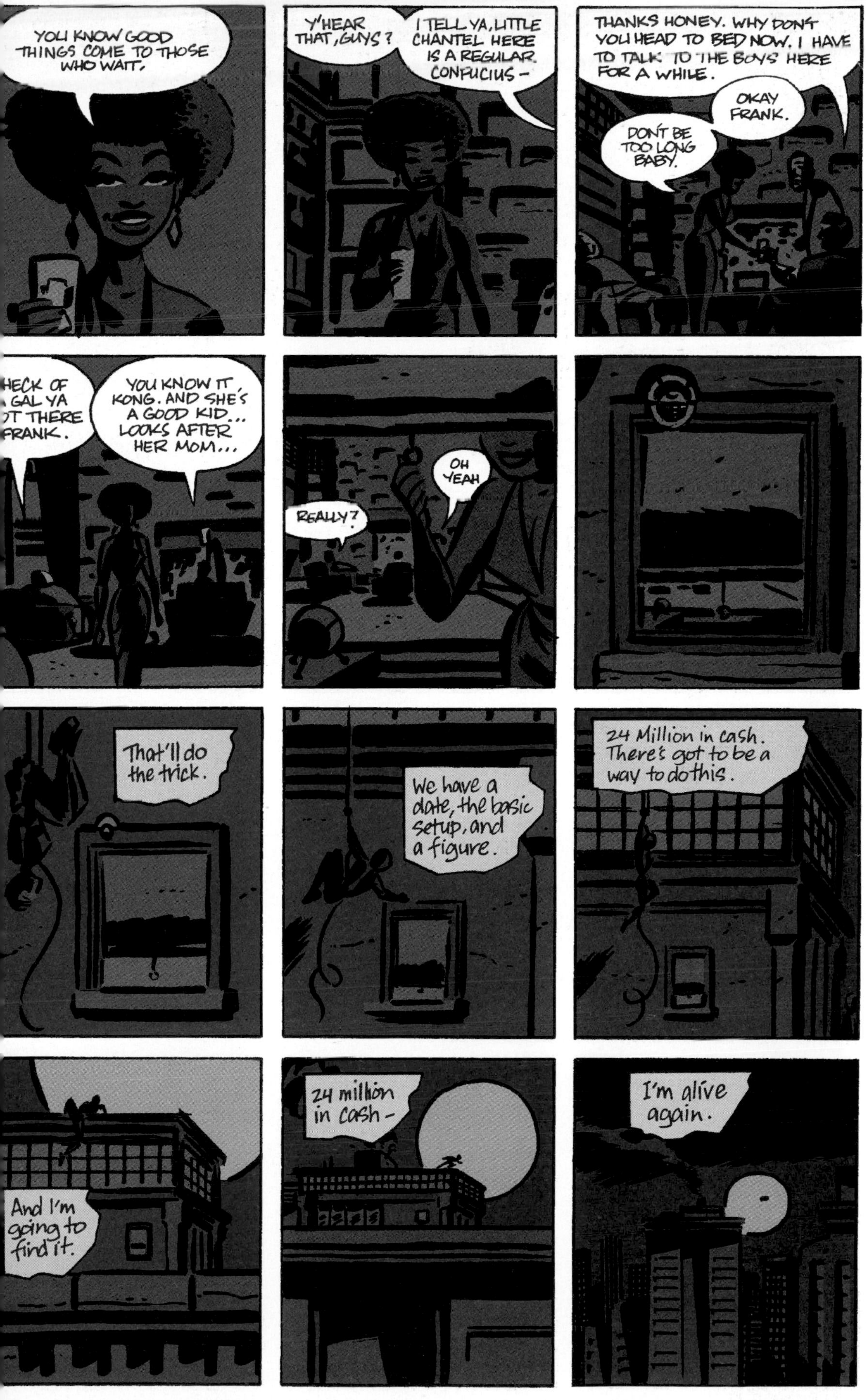
YOU KNOW GOOD THINGS COME TO THOSE WHO WAIT.
Y'HEAR THAT, GUYS?
I TELL YA, LITTLE CHANTEL HERE IS A REGULAR CONFUCIUS –
THANKS HONEY. WHY DON'T YOU HEAD TO BED NOW. I HAVE TO TALK TO THE BOYS HERE FOR A WHILE.
OKAY FRANK.
DON'T BE TOO LONG BABY.
HECK OF A GAL YA GOT THERE FRANK.
YOU KNOW IT, KONG. AND SHE'S A GOOD KID... LOOKS AFTER HER MOM...
OH YEAH
REALLY?
That'll do the trick.
We have a date, the basic setup, and a figure.
24 Million in cash. There's got to be a way to do this.
And I'm going to find it.
24 million in cash –
I'm alive again.

BOOK TWO
STARK

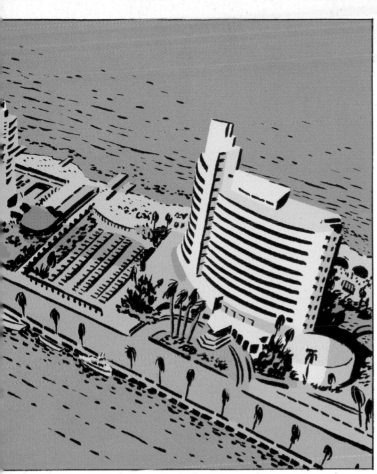

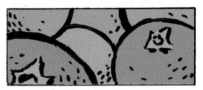

MIAMI BEACH

REFRESHES!

COMPLETELY AIR CONDITIONED SURFSIDE POOL

PRIVATE BEACH

FREE

THEY SAY THAT MIAMI IS FULL OF OLD PEOPLE AND GANGSTERS. I GUESS THAT THESE DAYS, I QUALIFY ON BOTH COUNTS.

EBB

FREE CABLE

TIDE

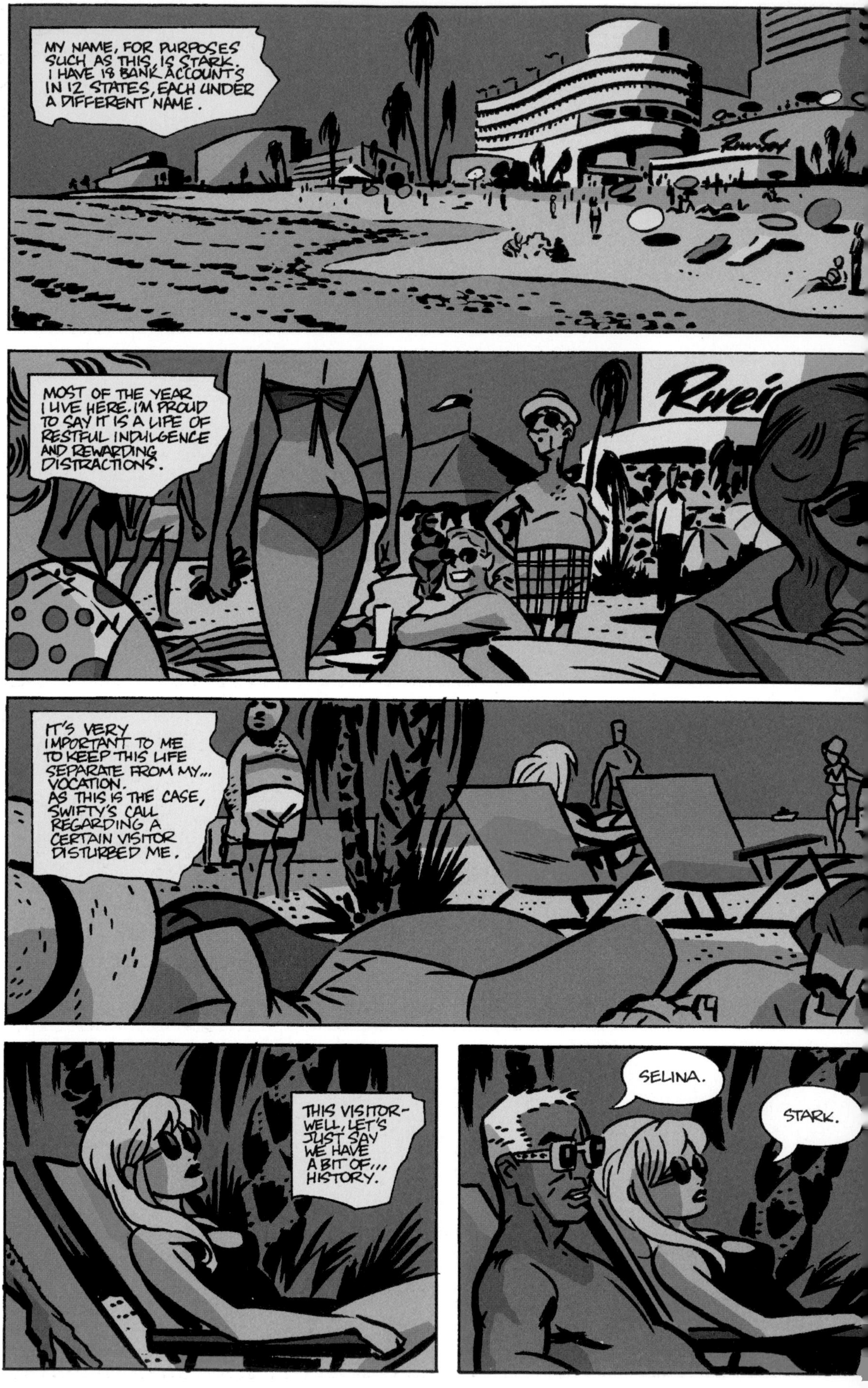

MY NAME, FOR PURPOSES SUCH AS THIS, IS STARK. I HAVE 18 BANK ACCOUNTS IN 12 STATES, EACH UNDER A DIFFERENT NAME.
MOST OF THE YEAR I LIVE HERE. I'M PROUD TO SAY IT IS A LIFE OF RESTFUL INDULGENCE AND REWARDING DISTRACTIONS.
IT'S VERY IMPORTANT TO ME TO KEEP THIS LIFE SEPARATE FROM MY... VOCATION. AS THIS IS THE CASE, SWIFTY'S CALL REGARDING A CERTAIN VISITOR DISTURBED ME.
THIS VISITOR-- WELL, LET'S JUST SAY WE HAVE A BIT OF... HISTORY.
SELINA.
STARK.

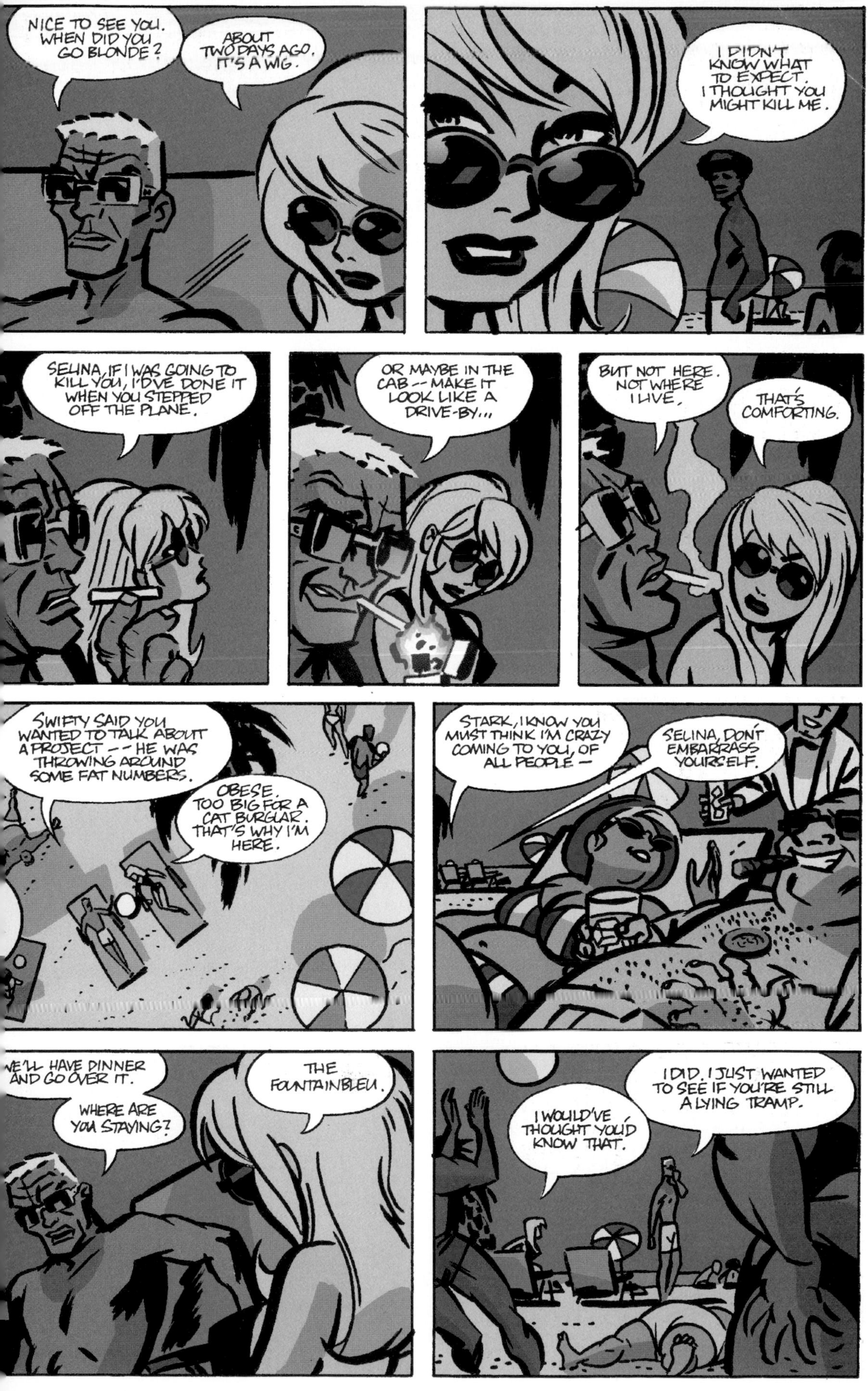
NICE TO SEE YOU. WHEN DID YOU GO BLONDE?
ABOUT TWO DAYS AGO. IT'S A WIG.
I DIDN'T KNOW WHAT TO EXPECT. I THOUGHT YOU MIGHT KILL ME.
SELINA, IF I WAS GOING TO KILL YOU, I'D'VE DONE IT WHEN YOU STEPPED OFF THE PLANE.
OR MAYBE IN THE CAB -- MAKE IT LOOK LIKE A DRIVE-BY...
BUT NOT HERE. NOT WHERE I LIVE.
THAT'S COMFORTING.
SWIFTY SAID YOU WANTED TO TALK ABOUT A PROJECT -- HE WAS THROWING AROUND SOME FAT NUMBERS.
OBESE. TOO BIG FOR A CAT BURGLAR. THAT'S WHY I'M HERE.
STARK, I KNOW YOU MUST THINK I'M CRAZY COMING TO YOU, OF ALL PEOPLE --
SELINA, DON'T EMBARRASS YOURSELF.
WE'LL HAVE DINNER AND GO OVER IT.
WHERE ARE YOU STAYING?
THE FOUNTAINBLEU.
I WOULD'VE THOUGHT YOU'D KNOW THAT.
I DID. I JUST WANTED TO SEE IF YOU'RE STILL A LYING TRAMP.

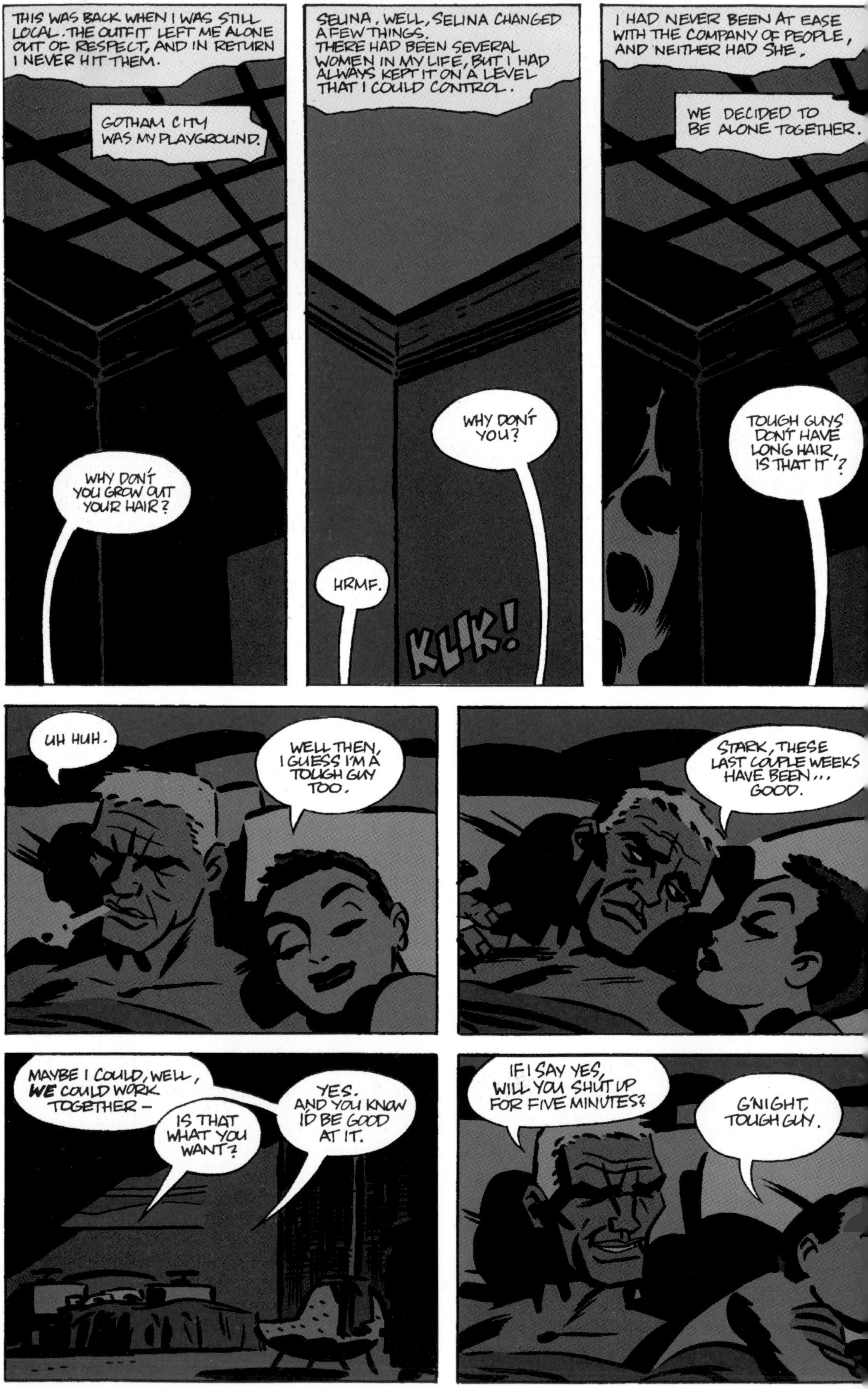
THIS WAS BACK WHEN I WAS STILL LOCAL. THE OUTFIT LEFT ME ALONE OUT OF RESPECT, AND IN RETURN I NEVER HIT THEM.
GOTHAM CITY WAS MY PLAYGROUND.
WHY DON'T YOU GROW OUT YOUR HAIR?
SELINA, WELL, SELINA CHANGED A FEW THINGS. THERE HAD BEEN SEVERAL WOMEN IN MY LIFE, BUT I HAD ALWAYS KEPT IT ON A LEVEL THAT I COULD CONTROL.
WHY DON'T YOU?
HRMF.
KLIK!
I HAD NEVER BEEN AT EASE WITH THE COMPANY OF PEOPLE, AND NEITHER HAD SHE.
WE DECIDED TO BE ALONE TOGETHER.
TOUGH GUYS DON'T HAVE LONG HAIR, IS THAT IT?
UH HUH.
WELL THEN, I GUESS I'M A TOUGH GUY TOO.
STARK, THESE LAST COUPLE WEEKS HAVE BEEN... GOOD.
MAYBE I COULD, WELL, WE COULD WORK TOGETHER—
IS THAT WHAT YOU WANT?
YES. AND YOU KNOW I'D BE GOOD AT IT.
IF I SAY YES, WILL YOU SHUT UP FOR FIVE MINUTES?
G'NIGHT, TOUGH GUY.

SO I TAUGHT HER THE BASICS. BUT SELINA HAD HER OWN STYLE. THAT WOMAN WAS ALL ABOUT FINESSE. LIKE, ON A BOX JOB, I'LL GO WITH DYNAMITE OR PLASTIQUE. SELINA HAD TO MASTER THE HARD WAY.

I TAUGHT HER ABOUT WHAT WAS WORTH STEALING, BUT MORE IMPORTANTLY, WHAT NOT TO STEAL. HOW TO SPOT TROUBLE BEFORE IT HAPPENS AND HOW TO COVER YOUR TRACKS. SHE SOAKED IT IN...

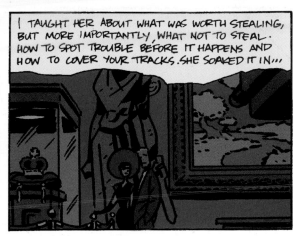

SHE HAD A JOB IN MIND. IT WAS A SIMPLE HEIST WITH MILLIONS IN UNCUT DIAMONDS... IT WAS A GREAT SET-UP...

...EXCEPT THE DIAMONDS BELONGED TO THE MOB.

I KNOW ABOUT THE MOB, BUT THIS IS MILLIONS IN UNCUT DIAMONDS JUST WAITING TO BE SNATCHED—

IT COULD BE OUR WAY OUT. Y'KNOW, DISAPPEAR. YOU AND I, ALONE TOGETHER.

OKAY. WE'LL LOOK AT IT.

AND THAT WAS MY FIRST MISTAKE. I LET THE POTENTIAL PAYOFF ON A JOB COMPROMISE MY GOLDEN RULE—DON'T SCREW WITH THE ITALIANS.

THAT WAS THEN.

STARK?

AND THAT IS THE NOW.

EARTH TO STARK!

27

SO THE QUESTION BECOMES WHETHER I'M JUST LISTENING TO HER PLAY ME ALL OVER AGAIN. I LET HER TALK, GET HER HOPES UP...

AND THERE ISN'T THAT MUCH TIME. IT GOES DOWN IN THREE WEEKS.

WHO'S THE INSIDE PERSON?

IT'S A WORKING GIRL. HER NAME'S NONE OF YOUR BUSINESS, BUT I TRUST HER, SHE'LL STAND UP.

TRUST. FORTUNATELY FOR YOU, IT DOESN'T COME DOWN TO TRUST.

LET'S STICK TO SOMETHING MORE CONCRETE-- LIKE COMMON SENSE.

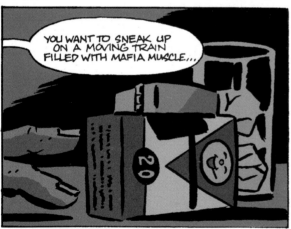

YOU WANT TO SNEAK UP ON A MOVING TRAIN FILLED WITH MAFIA MUSCLE...

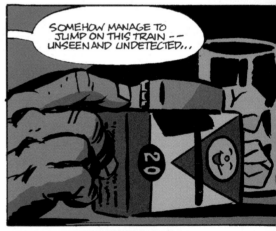

SOMEHOW MANAGE TO JUMP ON THIS TRAIN -- UNSEEN AND UNDETECTED...

AND WHAT DO WE DO THEN? DO WE FLY AWAY WITH THE MONEY IN OUR POCKETS?

BABY, YOU WERE GOOD, BUT YOU WERE NEVER THAT GOOD.

28

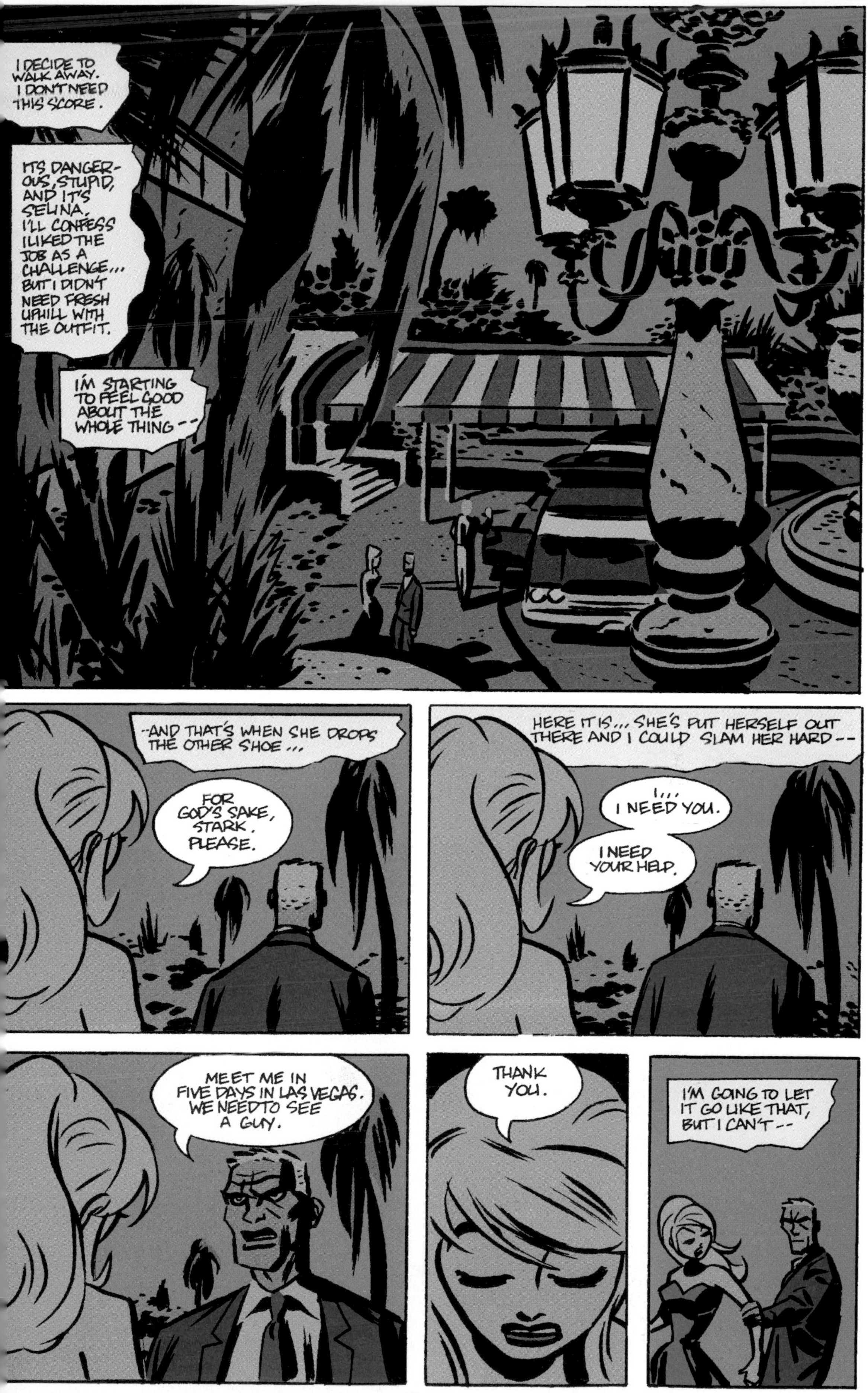
I DECIDE TO WALK AWAY. I DON'T NEED THIS SCORE.
IT'S DANGEROUS, STUPID, AND IT'S SELINA. I'LL CONFESS I LIKED THE JOB AS A CHALLENGE... BUT I DIDN'T NEED FRESH UPHILL WITH THE OUTFIT.
I'M STARTING TO FEEL GOOD ABOUT THE WHOLE THING --
-- AND THAT'S WHEN SHE DROPS THE OTHER SHOE...
FOR GOD'S SAKE, STARK. PLEASE.
HERE IT IS... SHE'S PUT HERSELF OUT THERE AND I COULD SLAM HER HARD --
I... I NEED YOU.
I NEED YOUR HELP.
MEET ME IN FIVE DAYS IN LAS VEGAS. WE NEED TO SEE A GUY.
THANK YOU.
I'M GOING TO LET IT GO LIKE THAT, BUT I CAN'T --

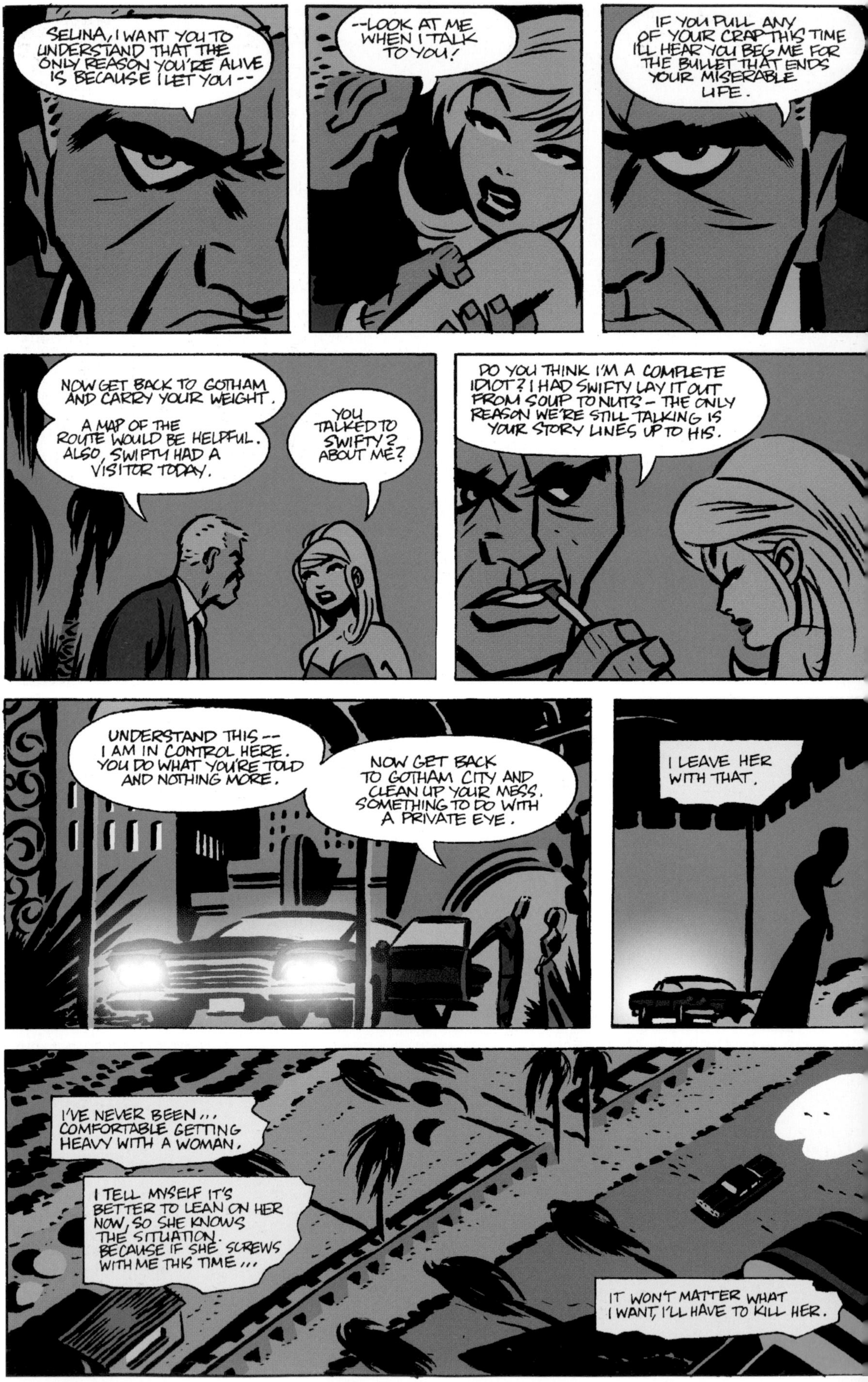

SELINA, I WANT YOU TO UNDERSTAND THAT THE ONLY REASON YOU'RE ALIVE IS BECAUSE I LET YOU --
--LOOK AT ME WHEN I TALK TO YOU!
IF YOU PULL ANY OF YOUR CRAP THIS TIME I'LL HEAR YOU BEG ME FOR THE BULLET THAT ENDS YOUR MISERABLE LIFE.
NOW GET BACK TO GOTHAM AND CARRY YOUR WEIGHT.
A MAP OF THE ROUTE WOULD BE HELPFUL. ALSO, SWIFTY HAD A VISITOR TODAY.
YOU TALKED TO SWIFTY? ABOUT ME?
DO YOU THINK I'M A COMPLETE IDIOT? I HAD SWIFTY LAY IT OUT FROM SOUP TO NUTS -- THE ONLY REASON WE'RE STILL TALKING IS YOUR STORY LINES UP TO HIS.
UNDERSTAND THIS -- I AM IN CONTROL HERE. YOU DO WHAT YOU'RE TOLD AND NOTHING MORE.
NOW GET BACK TO GOTHAM CITY AND CLEAN UP YOUR MESS. SOMETHING TO DO WITH A PRIVATE EYE.
I LEAVE HER WITH THAT.
I'VE NEVER BEEN... COMFORTABLE GETTING HEAVY WITH A WOMAN.
I TELL MYSELF IT'S BETTER TO LEAN ON HER NOW, SO SHE KNOWS THE SITUATION. BECAUSE IF SHE SCREWS WITH ME THIS TIME...
IT WON'T MATTER WHAT I WANT, I'LL HAVE TO KILL HER.

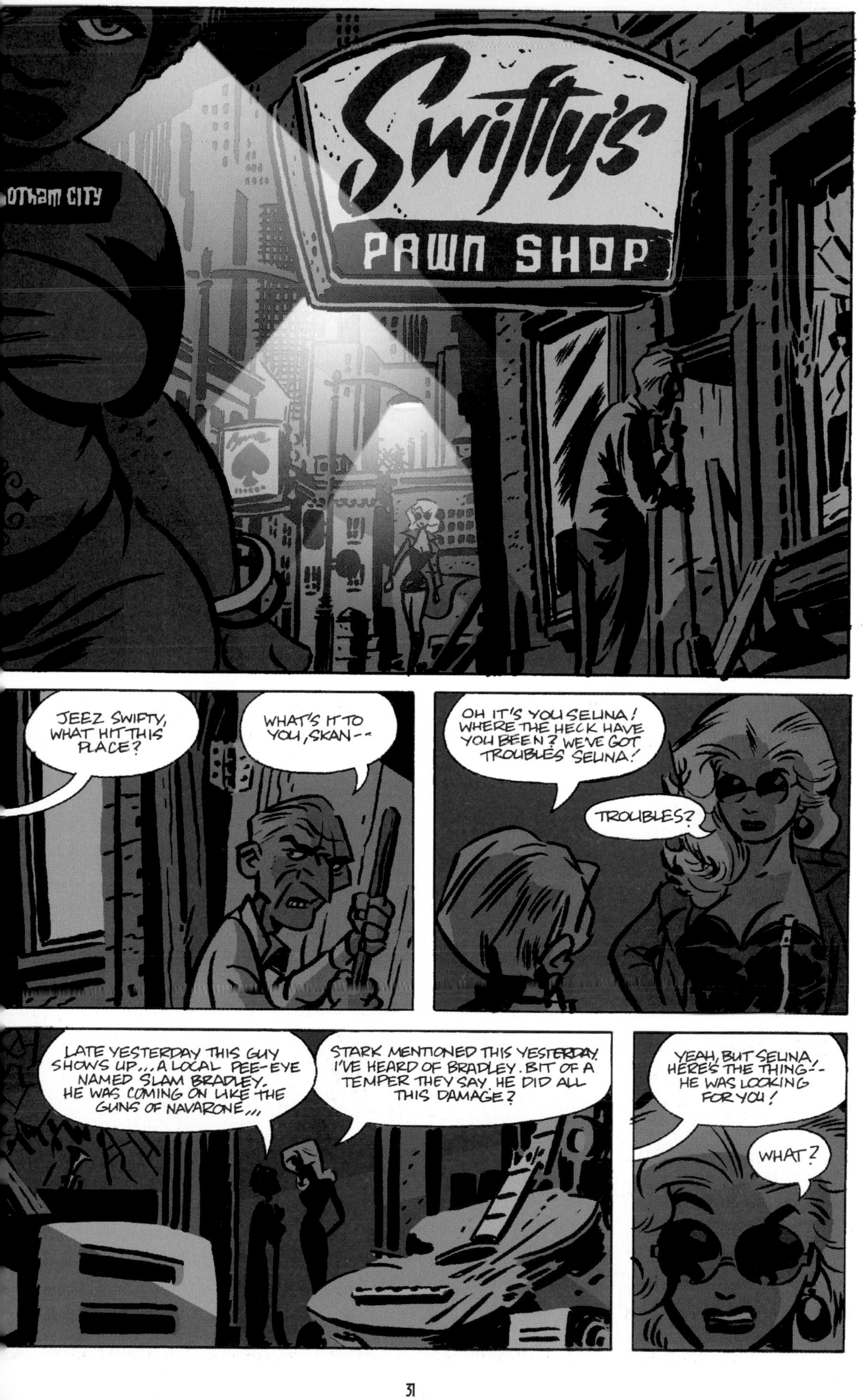
Swifty's
PAWN SHOP
OTHAM CITY
JEEZ SWIFTY, WHAT HIT THIS PLACE?
WHAT'S IT TO YOU, SKAN--
OH IT'S YOU SELINA! WHERE THE HECK HAVE YOU BEEN? WE'VE GOT TROUBLES SELINA!
TROUBLES?
LATE YESTERDAY THIS GUY SHOWS UP... A LOCAL PEE-EYE NAMED SLAM BRADLEY. HE WAS COMING ON LIKE THE GUNS OF NAVARONE...
STARK MENTIONED THIS YESTERDAY. I'VE HEARD OF BRADLEY. BIT OF A TEMPER THEY SAY. HE DID ALL THIS DAMAGE?
YEAH, BUT SELINA, HERE'S THE THING!- HE WAS LOOKING FOR YOU!
WHAT?

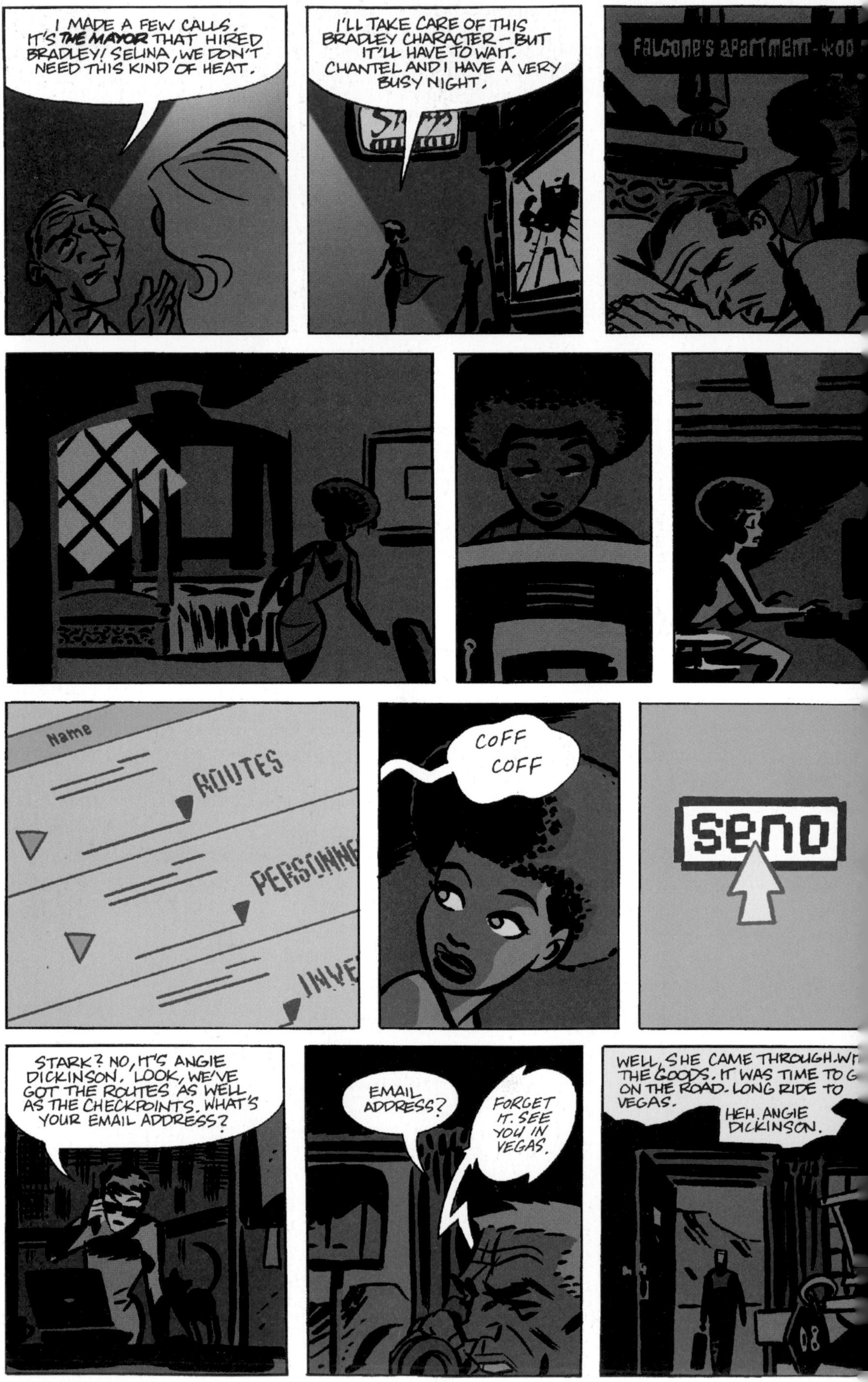
I MADE A FEW CALLS. IT'S THE MAYOR THAT HIRED BRADLEY! SELINA, WE DON'T NEED THIS KIND OF HEAT.
I'LL TAKE CARE OF THIS BRADLEY CHARACTER—BUT IT'LL HAVE TO WAIT. CHANTEL AND I HAVE A VERY BUSY NIGHT.
Falcone's apartment
Name
ROUTES
COFF COFF
SEND
STARK? NO, IT'S ANGIE DICKINSON. LOOK, WE'VE GOT THE ROUTES AS WELL AS THE CHECKPOINTS. WHAT'S YOUR EMAIL ADDRESS?
EMAIL ADDRESS?
FORGET IT. SEE YOU IN VEGAS.
WELL, SHE CAME THROUGH WI THE GOODS. IT WAS TIME TO G ON THE ROAD. LONG RIDE TO VEGAS.
HEH. ANGIE DICKINSON.

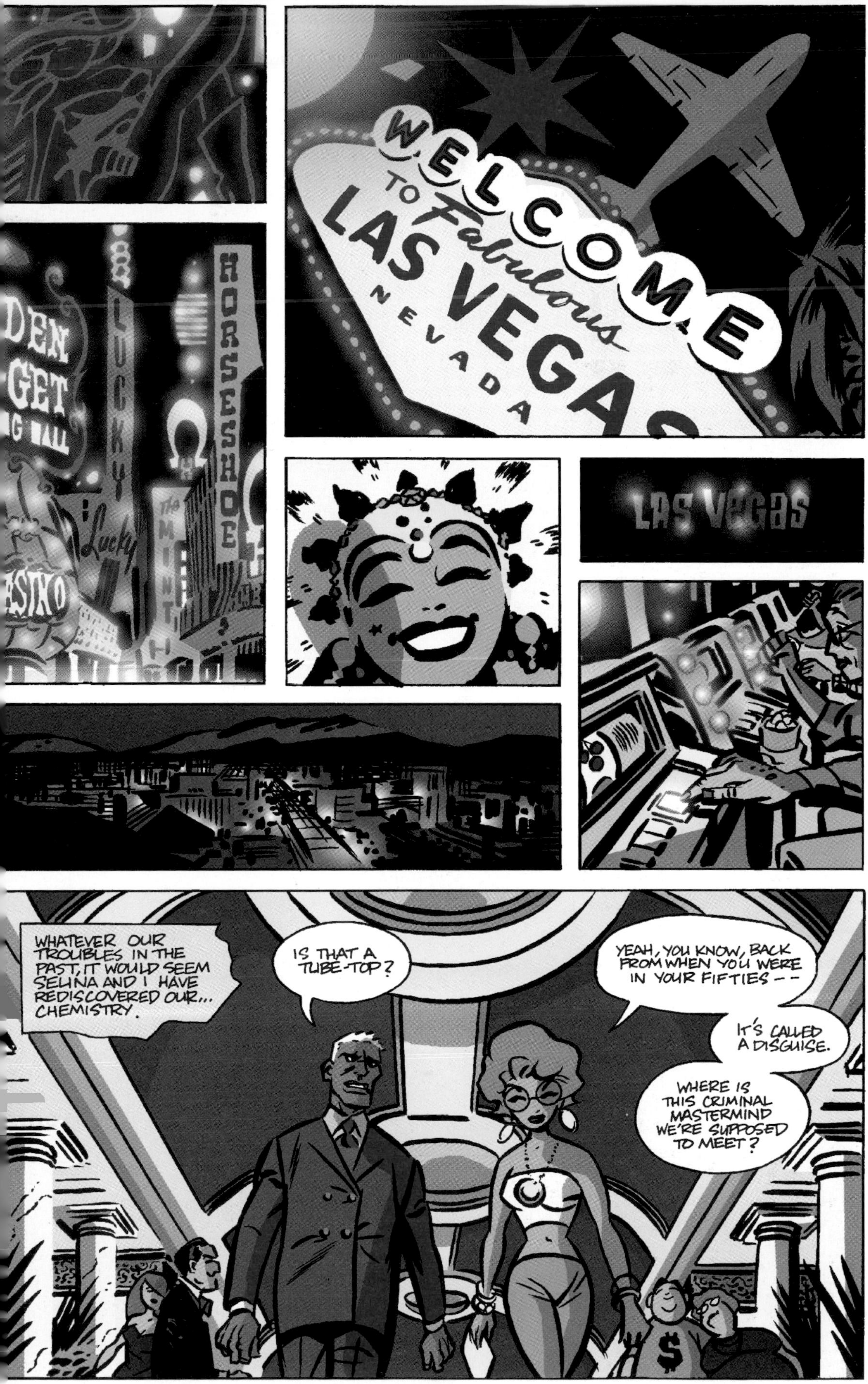

WELCOME TO Fabulous LAS VEGAS NEVADA
LUCKY
HORSESHOE
Lucky
The MINT
LAS VEGAS
WHATEVER OUR TROUBLES IN THE PAST, IT WOULD SEEM SELINA AND I HAVE REDISCOVERED OUR... CHEMISTRY.
IS THAT A TUBE-TOP?
YEAH, YOU KNOW, BACK FROM WHEN YOU WERE IN YOUR FIFTIES --
IT'S CALLED A DISGUISE.
WHERE IS THIS CRIMINAL MASTERMIND WE'RE SUPPOSED TO MEET?

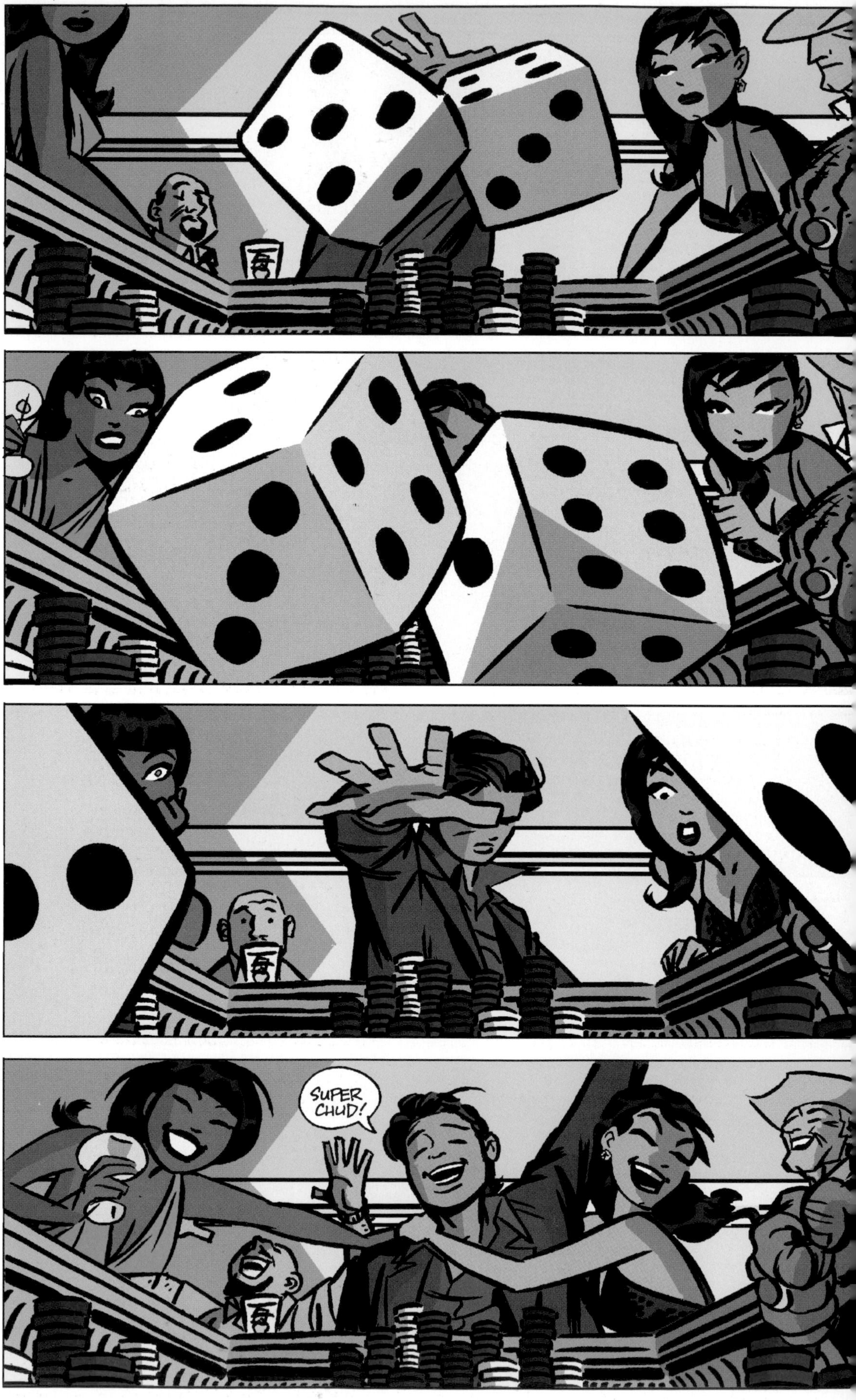
SUPER CHUD!

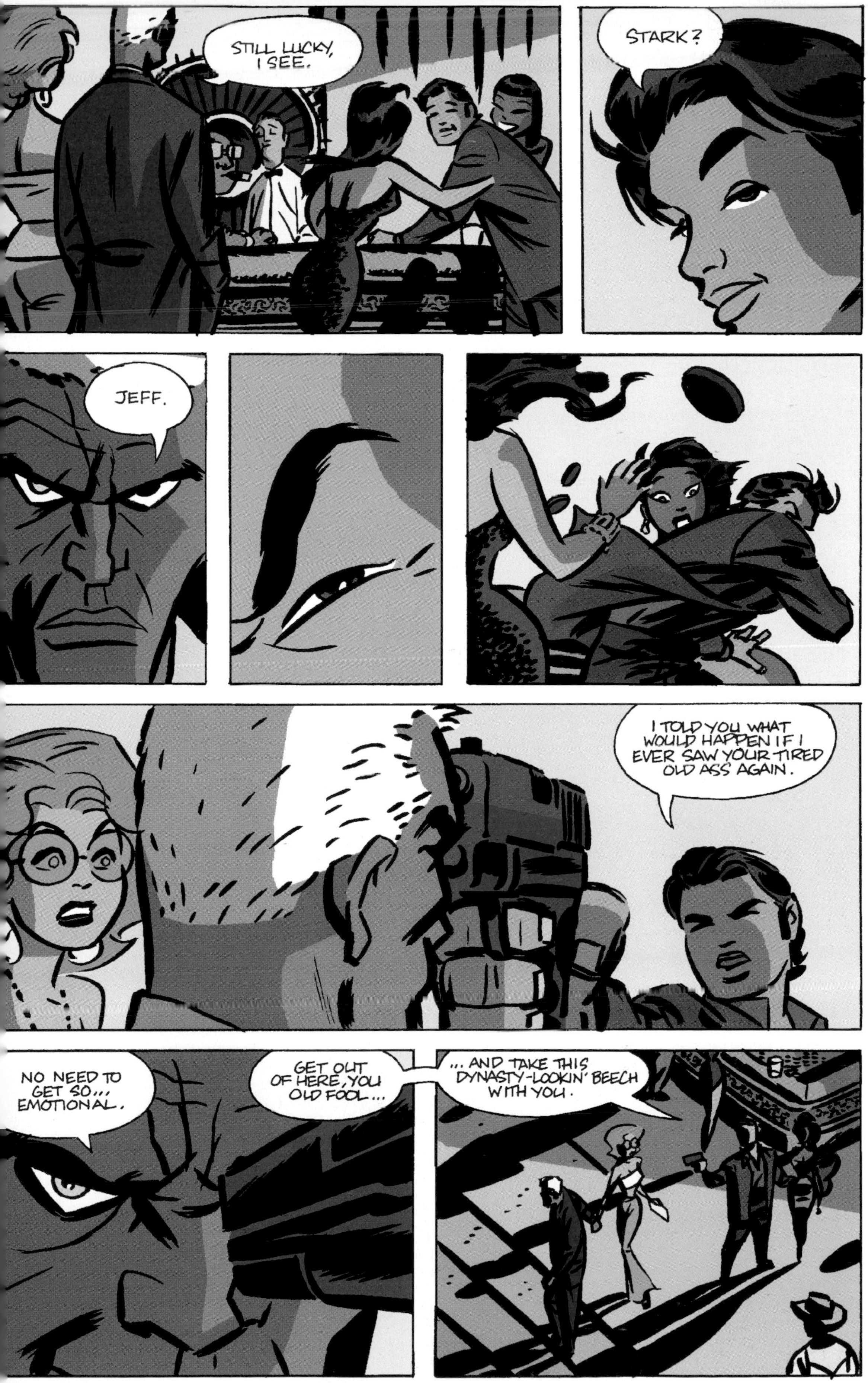
STILL LUCKY, I SEE.
STARK?
JEFF.
I TOLD YOU WHAT WOULD HAPPEN IF I EVER SAW YOUR TIRED OLD ASS AGAIN.
NO NEED TO GET SO... EMOTIONAL.
GET OUT OF HERE, YOU OLD FOOL...
... AND TAKE THIS DYNASTY-LOOKIN' BEECH WITH YOU.

I TAKE HER TO A DUMP ON FREEMONT. SHE DOESN'T KNOW THE PLAY SO I LET HER CARRY ON.

WHAT WAS I THINKING? IF THAT'S ANY INDICATION OF THE TYPE OF PEOPLE YOU WORK WITH...

I THOUGHT YOU'D HAVE THE SENSE TO MAKE SURE THIS WAS SOLID BEFORE WE--

WHAT DID I TELL YOU, OLD FOOL?

I DECIDED TO FOLLOW YOU AND FINISH THE JOB.

AHAHAHA!

WATCH OUT LADY! I THINK IT'S LOADED!

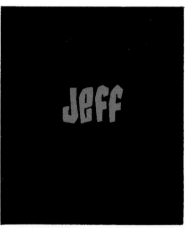
JEFF

SORRY ABOUT EARLIER. A COUPLE OF THOSE PLAYERS WERE CONNECTED, AND THE LAST THING WE NEED IS THEM THINKING THAT STARK AND I ARE UP TO SOMETHING.

SELINA, MEET JEFF.

DYNASTY-LOOKIN' BEECH?

MAYBE YOU NEED A POOL-BOY, HEY MAMA?

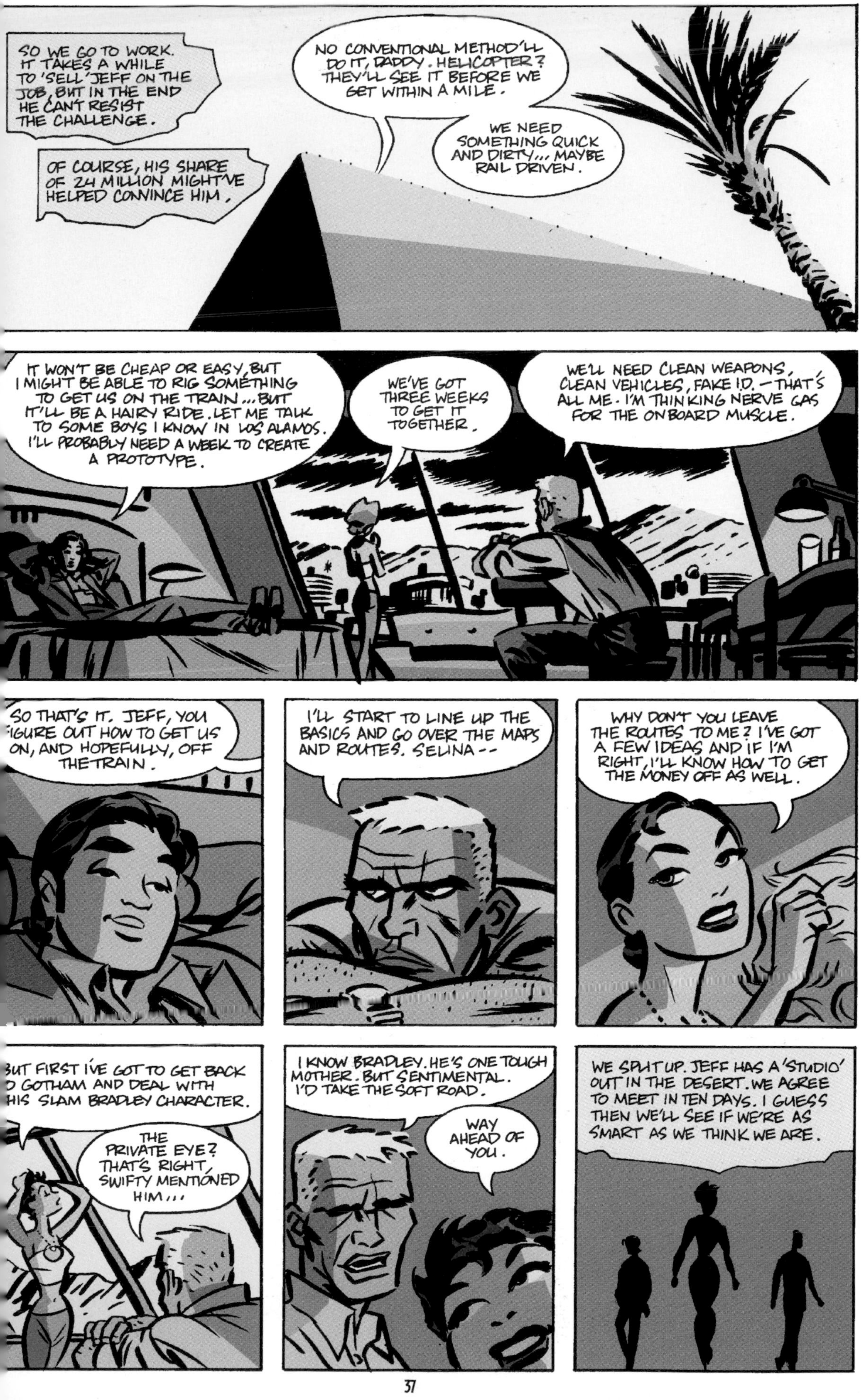
SO WE GO TO WORK. IT TAKES A WHILE TO 'SELL' JEFF ON THE JOB, BUT IN THE END HE CAN'T RESIST THE CHALLENGE.
OF COURSE, HIS SHARE OF 24 MILLION MIGHT'VE HELPED CONVINCE HIM.
NO CONVENTIONAL METHOD'LL DO IT, DADDY. HELICOPTER? THEY'LL SEE IT BEFORE WE GET WITHIN A MILE.
WE NEED SOMETHING QUICK AND DIRTY... MAYBE RAIL DRIVEN.
IT WON'T BE CHEAP OR EASY, BUT I MIGHT BE ABLE TO RIG SOMETHING TO GET US ON THE TRAIN... BUT IT'LL BE A HAIRY RIDE. LET ME TALK TO SOME BOYS I KNOW IN LOS ALAMOS. I'LL PROBABLY NEED A WEEK TO CREATE A PROTOTYPE.
WE'VE GOT THREE WEEKS TO GET IT TOGETHER.
WE'LL NEED CLEAN WEAPONS, CLEAN VEHICLES, FAKE I.D. — THAT'S ALL ME. I'M THINKING NERVE GAS FOR THE ONBOARD MUSCLE.
SO THAT'S IT. JEFF, YOU FIGURE OUT HOW TO GET US ON, AND HOPEFULLY, OFF THE TRAIN.
I'LL START TO LINE UP THE BASICS AND GO OVER THE MAPS AND ROUTES. SELINA--
WHY DON'T YOU LEAVE THE ROUTES TO ME? I'VE GOT A FEW IDEAS AND IF I'M RIGHT, I'LL KNOW HOW TO GET THE MONEY OFF AS WELL.
BUT FIRST I'VE GOT TO GET BACK TO GOTHAM AND DEAL WITH THIS SLAM BRADLEY CHARACTER.
THE PRIVATE EYE? THAT'S RIGHT, SWIFTY MENTIONED HIM...
I KNOW BRADLEY. HE'S ONE TOUGH MOTHER. BUT SENTIMENTAL. I'D TAKE THE SOFT ROAD.
WAY AHEAD OF YOU.
WE SPLIT UP. JEFF HAS A 'STUDIO' OUT IN THE DESERT. WE AGREE TO MEET IN TEN DAYS. I GUESS THEN WE'LL SEE IF WE'RE AS SMART AS WE THINK WE ARE.

DEATH VALLEY--FOUR DAYS LATER

SPORTS HEROES AND MOVIESTARS ASIDE, I LIVE IN WHAT COULD BE CONSIDERED A LAVISH FASHION.

BUT FOR ALL THE REWARDS, I NEVER FEEL MORE PEACE THAN WHEN I'M WORKING.

IN THE SERVICE I ENDED UP IN THE SIGNAL CORPS AND THEN SPECIAL OPS. I LEARNED TWO THINGS - HOW TO PLAN AND ACT UNDER PRESSURE ... AND HOW TO KILL.

SELINA AND JEFF ARE YOUNG AND MOTIVATED. I LEAVE THE CREATIVE THINKING TO THEM. CRAP, I JUST FOUND OUT WHAT EMAIL IS.

BUT IT'S NOT JUST THE SMASH AND GRAB - YOU HAVE TO HAVE A PLAN THAT COVERS YOUR OUT- TOO MANY COWBOYS DON'T THINK PAST GETTING THE MONEY IN THEIR HANDS.

TODAY I'M GOING TO SEE 'MOM' - NOT MY MOM - I WAS STATE-RAISED. DON'T EVEN KNOW MY REAL NAME. THIS 'MOM' IS AN ASSOCIATE OF MINE.

HIGH-TONED SON OF

38

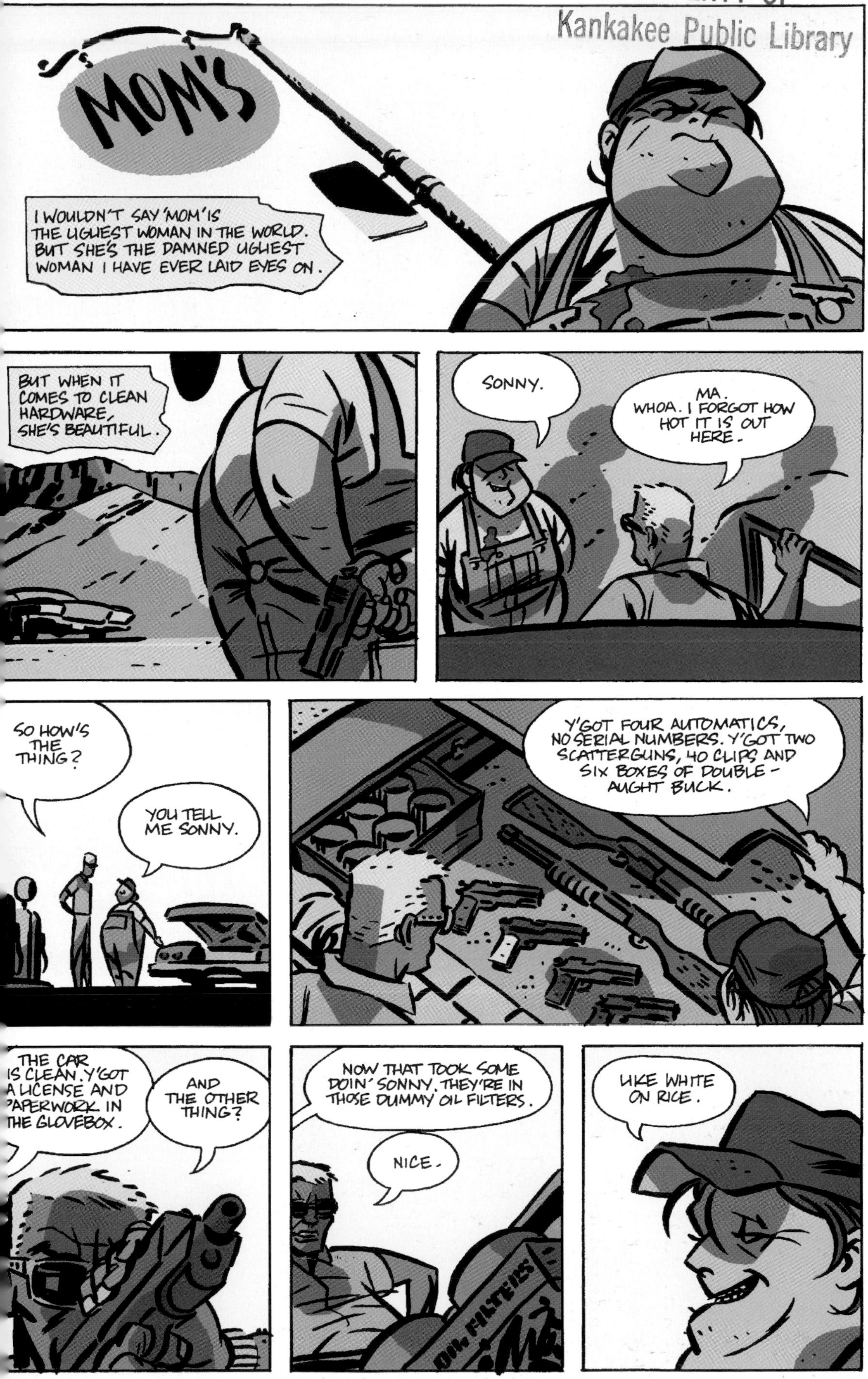
MOM'S
I WOULDN'T SAY 'MOM'IS THE UGLIEST WOMAN IN THE WORLD. BUT SHE'S THE DAMNED UGLIEST WOMAN I HAVE EVER LAID EYES ON.
BUT WHEN IT COMES TO CLEAN HARDWARE, SHE'S BEAUTIFUL.
SONNY.
MA. WHOA. I FORGOT HOW HOT IT IS OUT HERE.
SO HOW'S THE THING?
YOU TELL ME SONNY.
Y'GOT FOUR AUTOMATICS, NO SERIAL NUMBERS. Y'GOT TWO SCATTERGUNS, 40 CLIPS AND SIX BOXES OF DOUBLE-AUGHT BUCK.
THE CAR IS CLEAN. Y'GOT A LICENSE AND PAPERWORK IN THE GLOVEBOX.
AND THE OTHER THING?
NOW THAT TOOK SOME DOIN' SONNY. THEY'RE IN THOSE DUMMY OIL FILTERS.
NICE.
LIKE WHITE ON RICE.

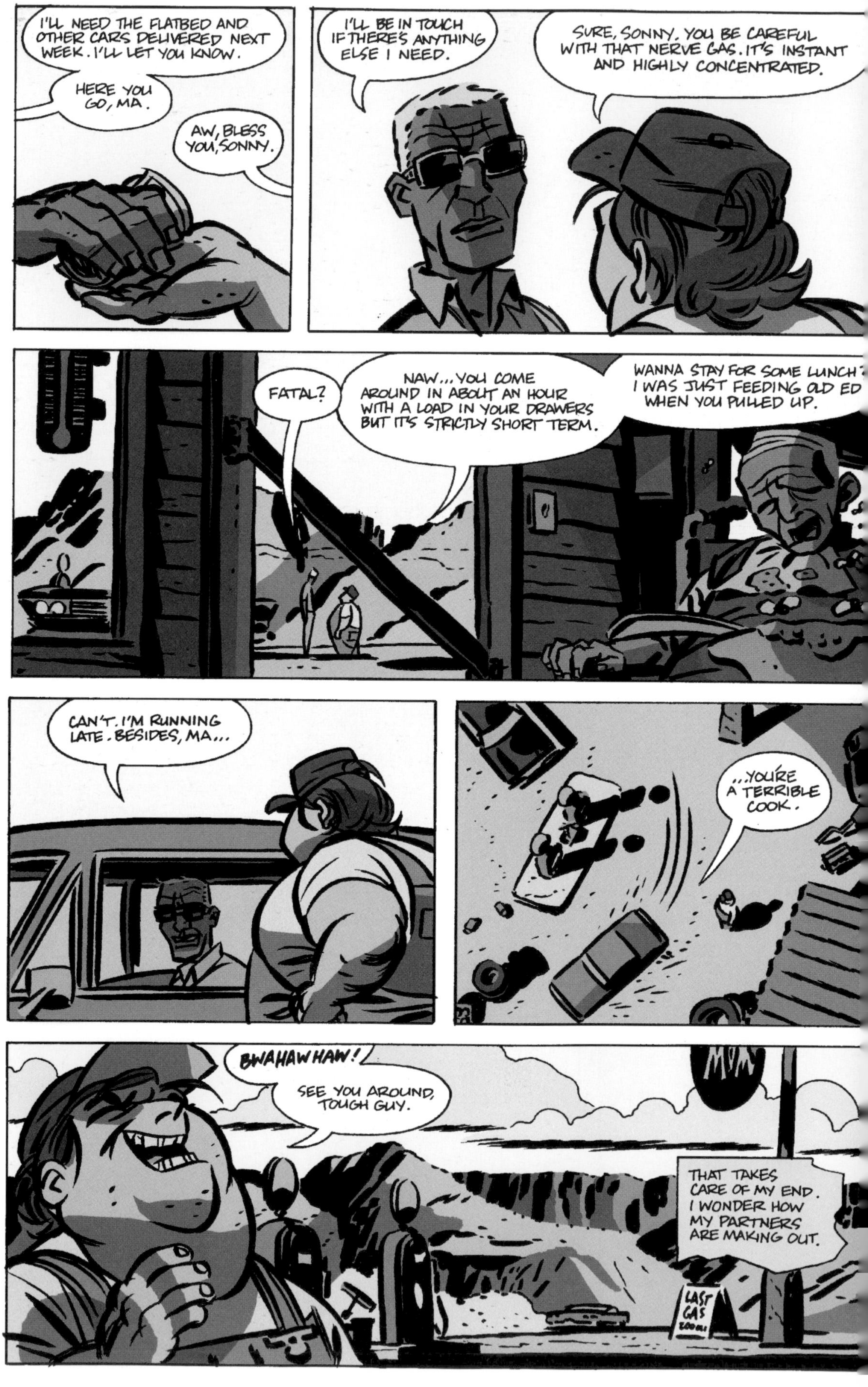
I'LL NEED THE FLATBED AND OTHER CARS DELIVERED NEXT WEEK. I'LL LET YOU KNOW.
HERE YOU GO, MA.
AW, BLESS YOU, SONNY.
I'LL BE IN TOUCH IF THERE'S ANYTHING ELSE I NEED.
SURE, SONNY. YOU BE CAREFUL WITH THAT NERVE GAS. IT'S INSTANT AND HIGHLY CONCENTRATED.
FATAL?
NAW... YOU COME AROUND IN ABOUT AN HOUR WITH A LOAD IN YOUR DRAWERS BUT IT'S STRICTLY SHORT TERM.
WANNA STAY FOR SOME LUNCH? I WAS JUST FEEDING OLD ED WHEN YOU PULLED UP.
CAN'T. I'M RUNNING LATE. BESIDES, MA...
...YOU'RE A TERRIBLE COOK.
BWAHAWHAW!
SEE YOU AROUND, TOUGH GUY.
THAT TAKES CARE OF MY END. I WONDER HOW MY PARTNERS ARE MAKING OUT.
LAST GAS

US AIR FORCE
20174

41

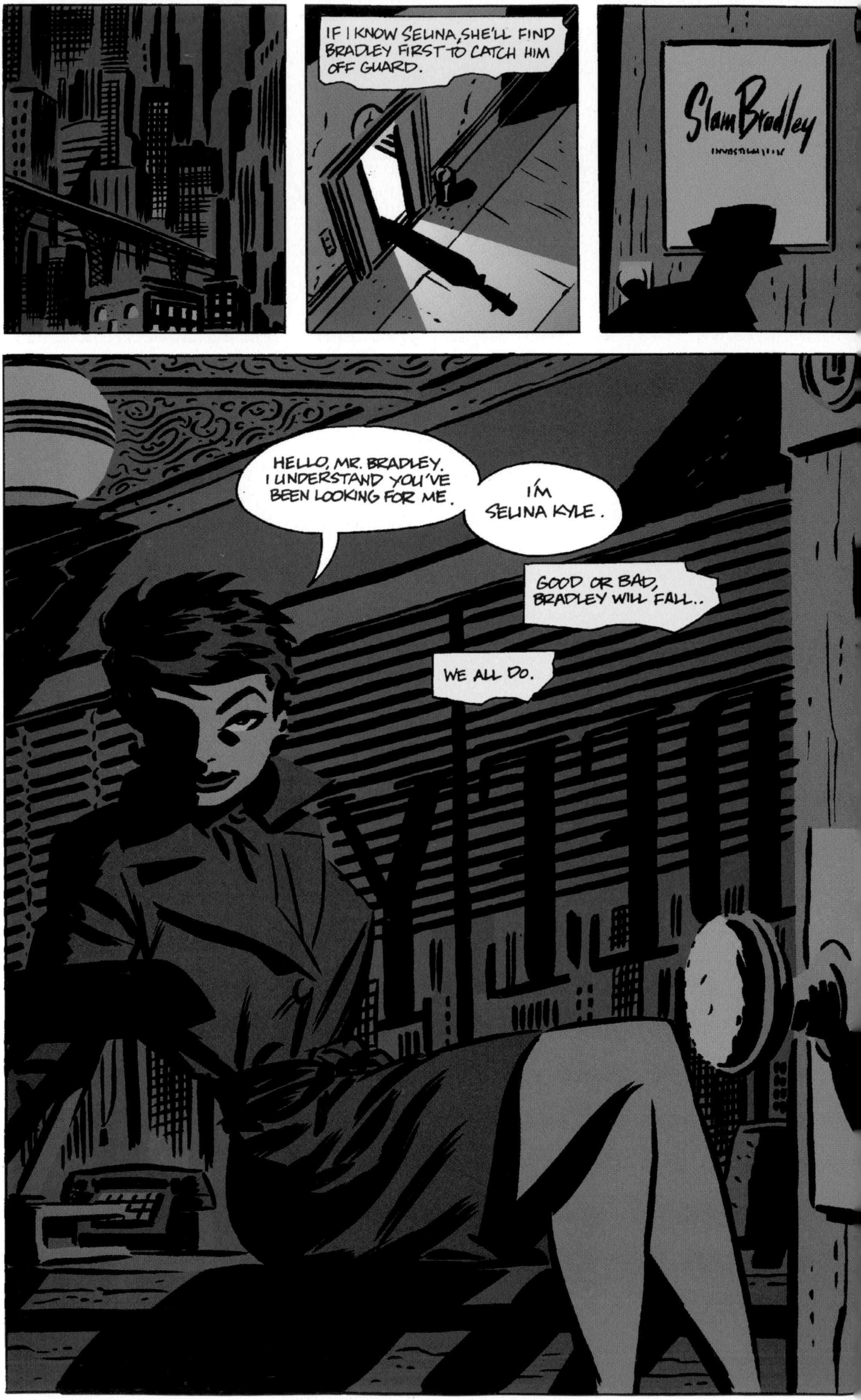
IF I KNOW SELINA, SHE'LL FIND BRADLEY FIRST TO CATCH HIM OFF GUARD.
Slam Bradley
HELLO, MR. BRADLEY. I UNDERSTAND YOU'VE BEEN LOOKING FOR ME.
I'M SELINA KYLE.
GOOD OR BAD, BRADLEY WILL FALL..
WE ALL DO.

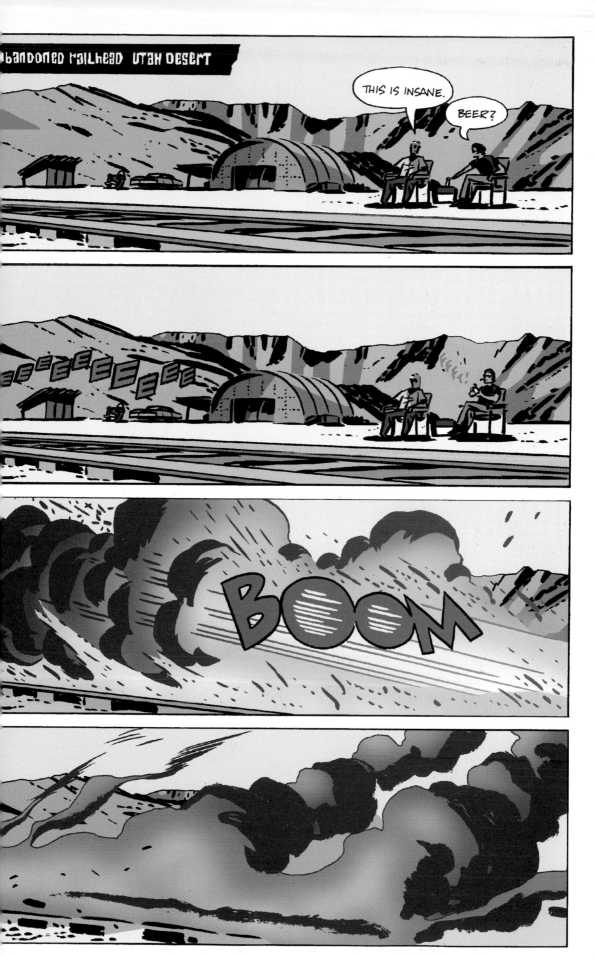

abandoned railhead utah desert

THIS IS INSANE.

BEER?

BOOM

43

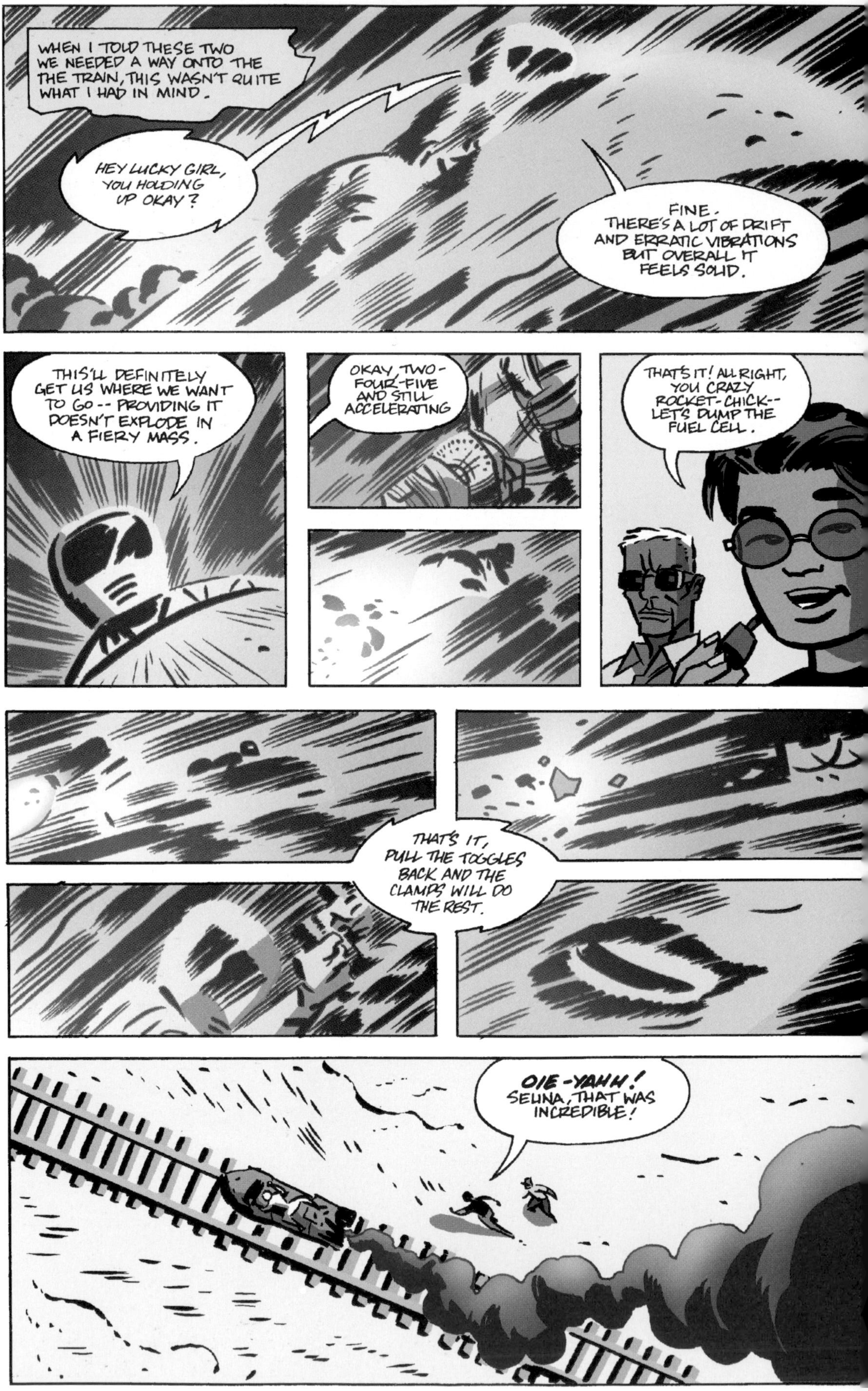
WHEN I TOLD THESE TWO WE NEEDED A WAY ONTO THE THE TRAIN, THIS WASN'T QUITE WHAT I HAD IN MIND.
HEY LUCKY GIRL, YOU HOLDING UP OKAY?
FINE. THERE'S A LOT OF DRIFT AND ERRATIC VIBRATIONS BUT OVERALL IT FEELS SOLID.
THIS'LL DEFINITELY GET US WHERE WE WANT TO GO -- PROVIDING IT DOESN'T EXPLODE IN A FIERY MASS.
OKAY, TWO-FOUR-FIVE AND STILL ACCELERATING
THAT'S IT! ALL RIGHT, YOU CRAZY ROCKET-CHICK-- LET'S DUMP THE FUEL CELL.
THAT'S IT, PULL THE TOGGLES BACK AND THE CLAMPS WILL DO THE REST.
OIE-YAHH! SELINA, THAT WAS INCREDIBLE!

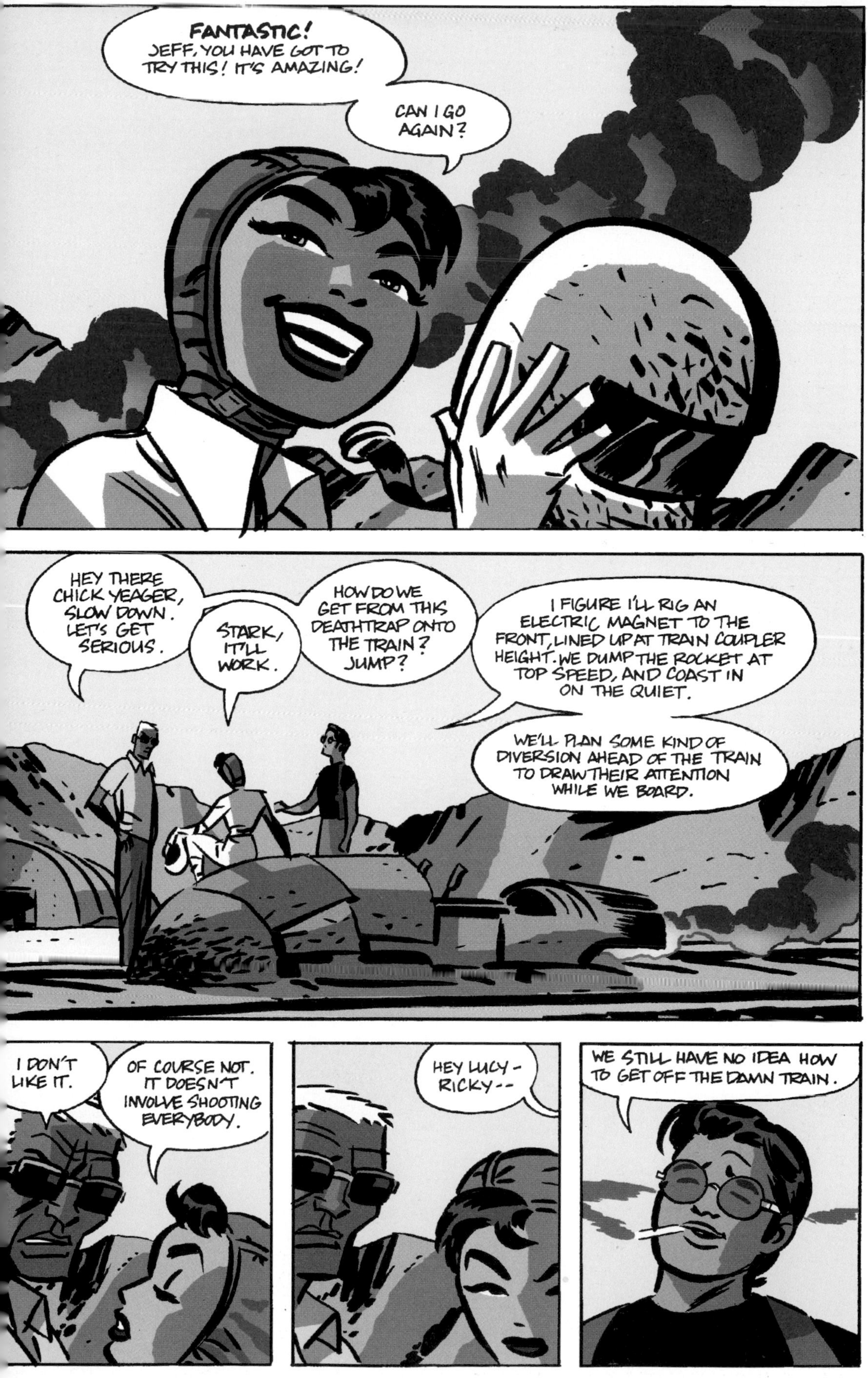
FANTASTIC! JEFF, YOU HAVE GOT TO TRY THIS! IT'S AMAZING!
CAN I GO AGAIN?
HEY THERE CHICK YEAGER, SLOW DOWN. LET'S GET SERIOUS.
STARK, IT'LL WORK.
HOW DO WE GET FROM THIS DEATHTRAP ONTO THE TRAIN? JUMP?
I FIGURE I'LL RIG AN ELECTRIC MAGNET TO THE FRONT, LINED UP AT TRAIN COUPLER HEIGHT. WE DUMP THE ROCKET AT TOP SPEED, AND COAST IN ON THE QUIET.
WE'LL PLAN SOME KIND OF DIVERSION AHEAD OF THE TRAIN TO DRAW THEIR ATTENTION WHILE WE BOARD.
I DON'T LIKE IT.
OF COURSE NOT. IT DOESN'T INVOLVE SHOOTING EVERYBODY.
HEY LUCY - RICKY --
WE STILL HAVE NO IDEA HOW TO GET OFF THE DAMN TRAIN.

THAT'S WHEN SELINA GETS A LOOK IN HER EYES AND HAS US FOLLOW HER INTO JEFF'S 'STUDIO! AT LEAST THAT'S WHAT JEFF CALLS IT. QUONSET HUT FULL OF CRAP IS MORE LIKE IT.

WHAT WE NEED IS A WAY OFF THE TRAIN AND A WAY TO HAUL 24 MILLION DOLLARS WORTH OF MONEYBAGS WITH US.

WITHOUT STOPPING THE TRAIN OR GETTING SHOT.

THANK YOU MR. POSITIVE. IF THE TRAIN NEVER STOPS THEY CAN'T PINPOINT WHERE THEY GOT HIT UNTIL WE'RE LONG GONE.

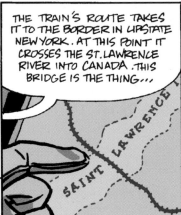

THE TRAIN'S ROUTE TAKES IT TO THE BORDER IN UPSTATE NEW YORK. AT THIS POINT IT CROSSES THE ST. LAWRENCE RIVER INTO CANADA. THIS BRIDGE IS THE THING...

SAINT LAWRENCE

IF WE BOARD RIGHT BEFORE THE BRIDGE AND GAS THE MUSCLE... WELL IT'S A PIECE OF CAKE, REALLY.

Y'SEEN THESE? INFLATABLE RAFT, ALL FOLDED UP WITH A CO² CHARGE? IF WE ATTACH THESE TO LENGTHS OF THIN CABLE LIKE SO --

WE LOOP THE CABLE THROUGH THE MONEYBAGS AND CLIP IT.

THEN DUMP THE 'DAISYCHAIN' OF MONEYBAGS OVER THE BRIDGE TO THE RIVER-- THE RAFTS INFLATE AND WE PICK 'EM UP BY BOAT.

SELINA FRIGGIN' KYLE.

IT'S... BRILLIANT.

WE'LL NEED A FOURTH FOR THE BOAT-- I WANT SWIFTY. I KNOW HE'S OLD BUT HE'S IN ON THIS ALREADY. PLUS, HE KNOWS HIS WAY AROUND A BOAT.

SWIFTY IS FINE KID. WE'LL NEED TO SPOT A COVE OR INLET OF SOME SORT TO HIDE THE BOAT.

46

I HATE TO BE THE SKIPPING CD, BUT HOW DO WE GET OFF THE TRAIN?

ISN'T IT OBVIOUS?

PARACHUTES.

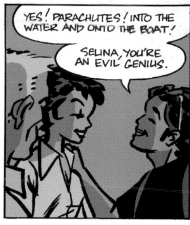

YES! PARACHUTES! INTO THE WATER AND ONTO THE BOAT!

SELINA, YOU'RE AN EVIL GENIUS.

WELL?

WHATTAYA SAY, HEY?

HEY.

OIE-YAH! LET'S GET FAT!

SELINA HAS TO HEAD BACK AND PREP SWIFTY, WHILE JEFF AND I NAIL DOWN THE BOAT THING. WE SEE HER OFF AND EVEN A BLIND MAN COULD TELL WHAT JEFF IS THINKING. FUNNY, BUT IT DOESN'T BOTHER ME.

JEALOUSY IS A WASTE OF TIME. AND IF THERE'S ONE THING I KNOW—

NOBODY OWNS SELINA.

47

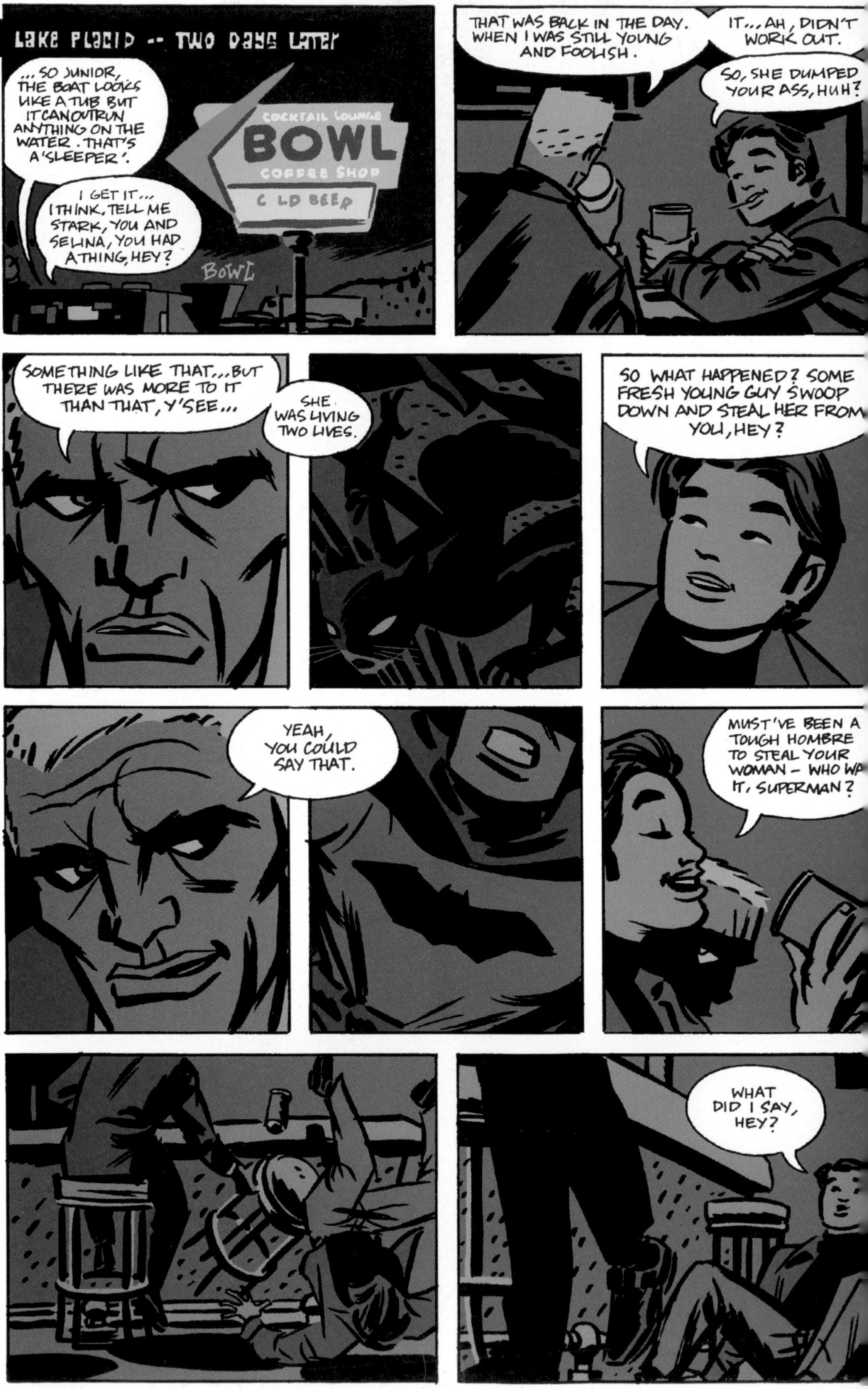
LAKE PLACID -- TWO DAYS LATER
...SO JUNIOR, THE BOAT LOOKS LIKE A TUB BUT IT CAN OUTRUN ANYTHING ON THE WATER. THAT'S A 'SLEEPER'.
COCKTAIL LOUNGE
BOWL
COFFEE SHOP
C LD BEER
I GET IT... I THINK. TELL ME STARK, YOU AND SELINA, YOU HAD A THING, HEY?
THAT WAS BACK IN THE DAY. WHEN I WAS STILL YOUNG AND FOOLISH.
IT... AH, DIDN'T WORK OUT.
SO, SHE DUMPED YOUR ASS, HUH?
SOMETHING LIKE THAT...BUT THERE WAS MORE TO IT THAN THAT, Y'SEE...
SHE WAS LIVING TWO LIVES.
SO WHAT HAPPENED? SOME FRESH YOUNG GUY SWOOP DOWN AND STEAL HER FROM YOU, HEY?
YEAH, YOU COULD SAY THAT.
MUST'VE BEEN A TOUGH HOMBRE TO STEAL YOUR WOMAN - WHO WA IT, SUPERMAN?
WHAT DID I SAY, HEY?

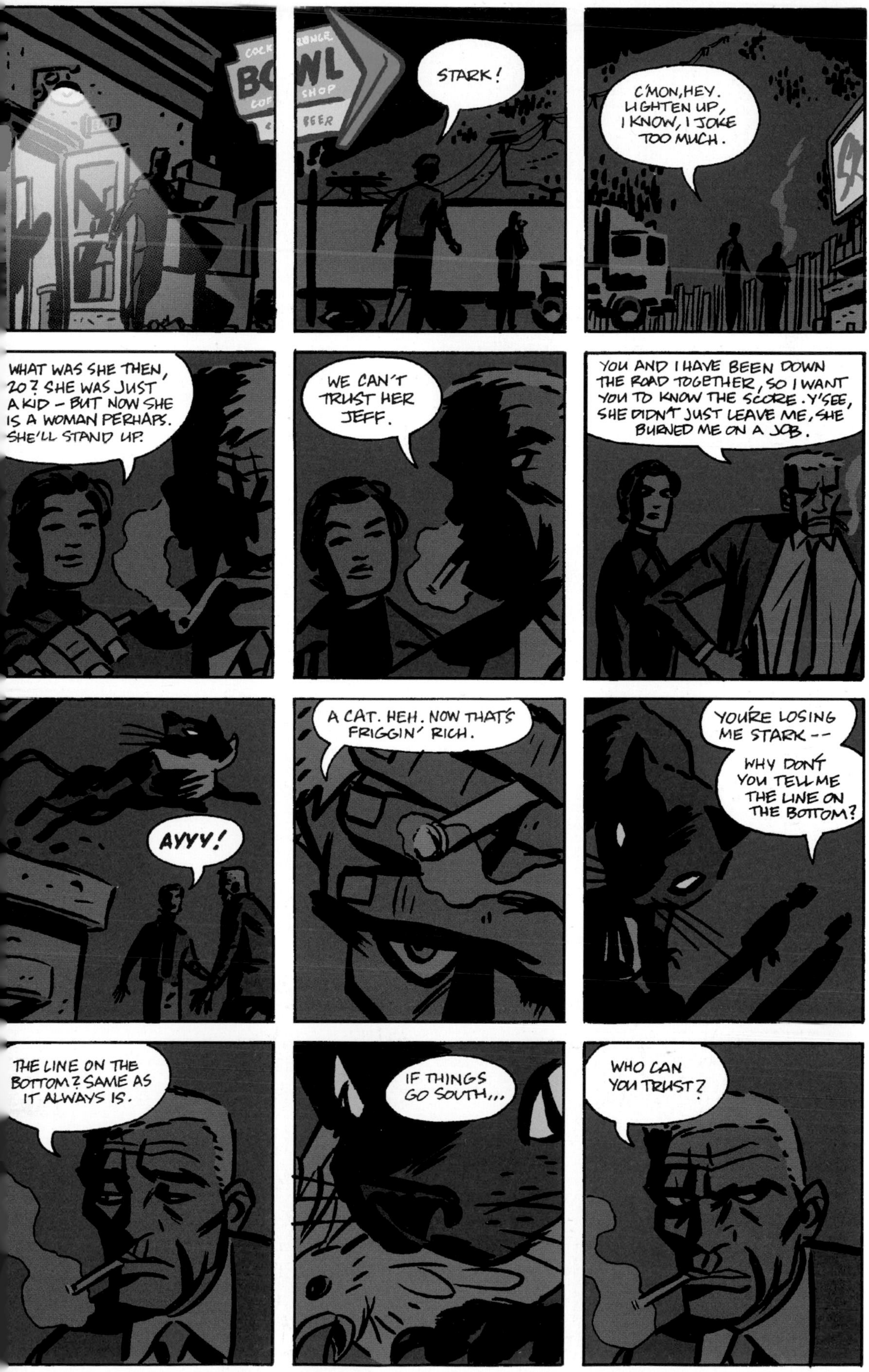
STARK!
C'MON, HEY. LIGHTEN UP, I KNOW, I JOKE TOO MUCH.
WHAT WAS SHE THEN, 20? SHE WAS JUST A KID - BUT NOW SHE IS A WOMAN PERHAPS. SHE'LL STAND UP.
WE CAN'T TRUST HER JEFF.
YOU AND I HAVE BEEN DOWN THE ROAD TOGETHER, SO I WANT YOU TO KNOW THE SCORE. Y'SEE, SHE DIDN'T JUST LEAVE ME, SHE BURNED ME ON A JOB.
AYYY!
A CAT. HEH. NOW THAT'S FRIGGIN' RICH.
YOU'RE LOSING ME STARK --
WHY DON'T YOU TELL ME THE LINE ON THE BOTTOM?
THE LINE ON THE BOTTOM? SAME AS IT ALWAYS IS.
IF THINGS GO SOUTH...
WHO CAN YOU TRUST?

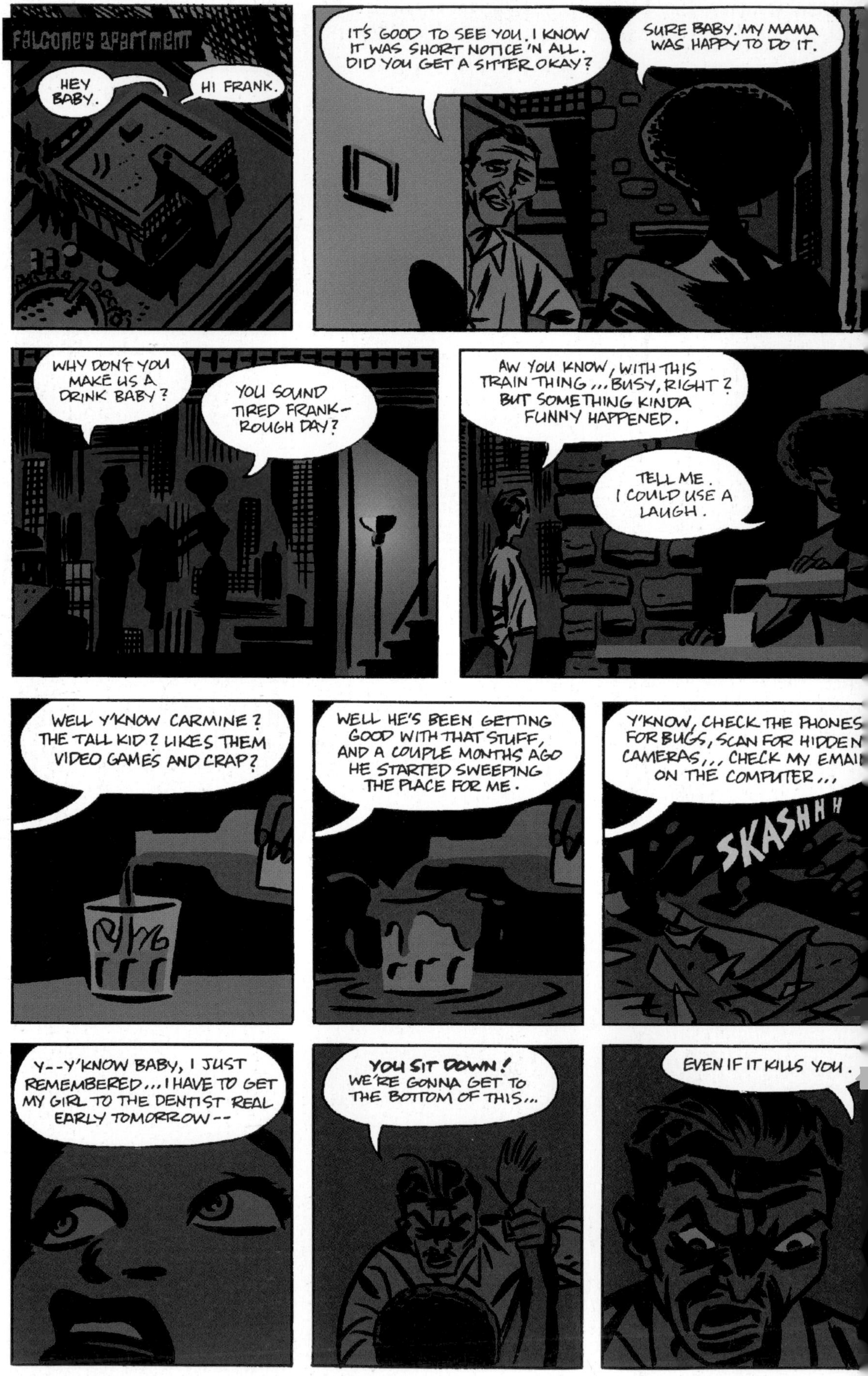
Falcone's apartment
HEY BABY.
HI FRANK.
IT'S GOOD TO SEE YOU. I KNOW IT WAS SHORT NOTICE 'N ALL. DID YOU GET A SITTER OKAY?
SURE BABY. MY MAMA WAS HAPPY TO DO IT.
WHY DON'T YOU MAKE US A DRINK BABY?
YOU SOUND TIRED FRANK-ROUGH DAY?
AW YOU KNOW, WITH THIS TRAIN THING,,, BUSY, RIGHT? BUT SOMETHING KINDA FUNNY HAPPENED.
TELL ME. I COULD USE A LAUGH.
WELL Y'KNOW CARMINE? THE TALL KID? LIKES THEM VIDEO GAMES AND CRAP?
WELL HE'S BEEN GETTING GOOD WITH THAT STUFF, AND A COUPLE MONTHS AGO HE STARTED SWEEPING THE PLACE FOR ME.
Y'KNOW, CHECK THE PHONES FOR BUGS, SCAN FOR HIDDEN CAMERAS,,, CHECK MY EMAIL ON THE COMPUTER,,,
SKASHHH
Y--Y'KNOW BABY, I JUST REMEMBERED... I HAVE TO GET MY GIRL TO THE DENTIST REAL EARLY TOMORROW--
YOU SIT DOWN! WE'RE GONNA GET TO THE BOTTOM OF THIS...
EVEN IF IT KILLS YOU.

BOOK THREE
SLAM

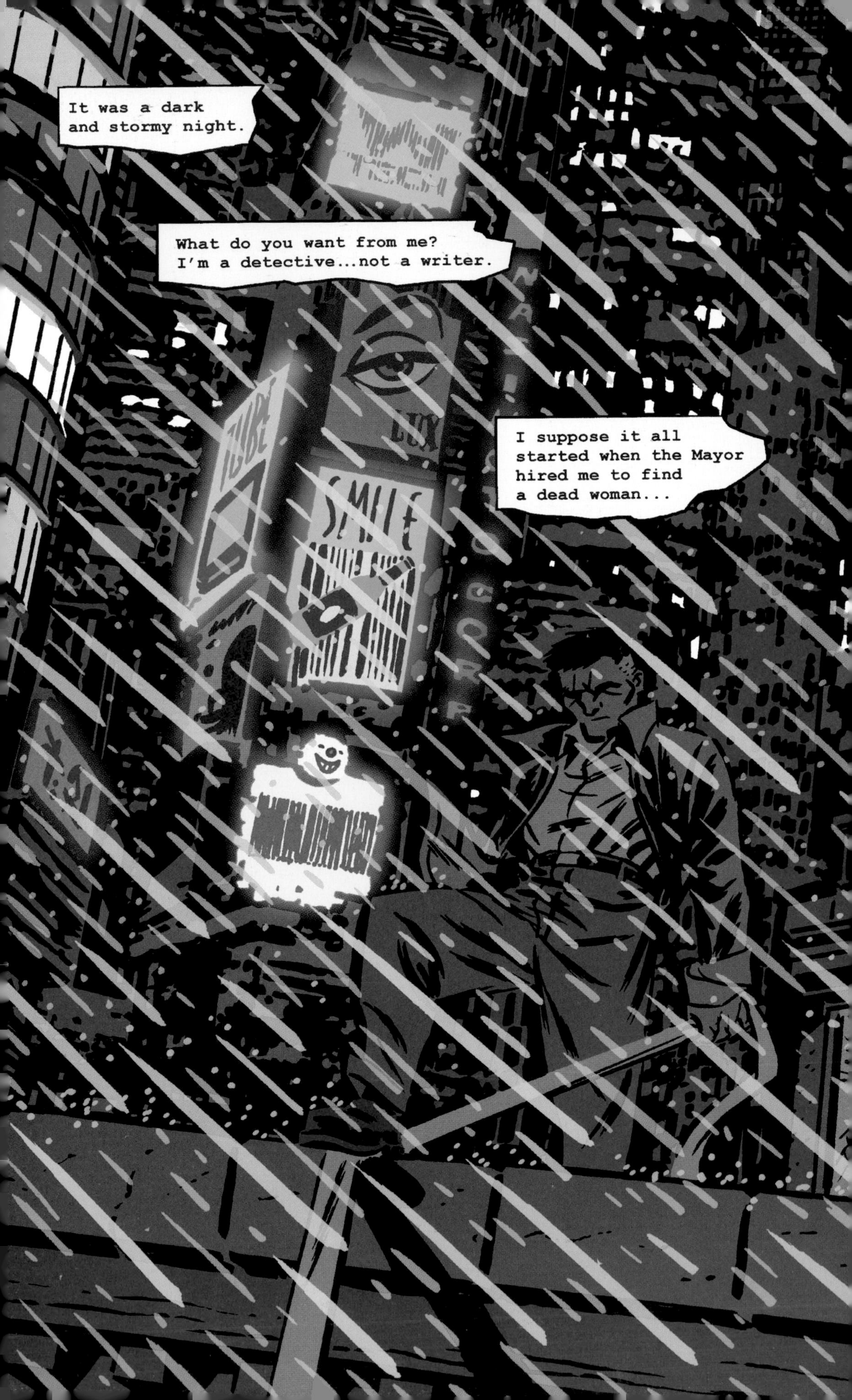
It was a dark and stormy night.
What do you want from me? I'm a detective...not a writer.
I suppose it all started when the Mayor hired me to find a dead woman...

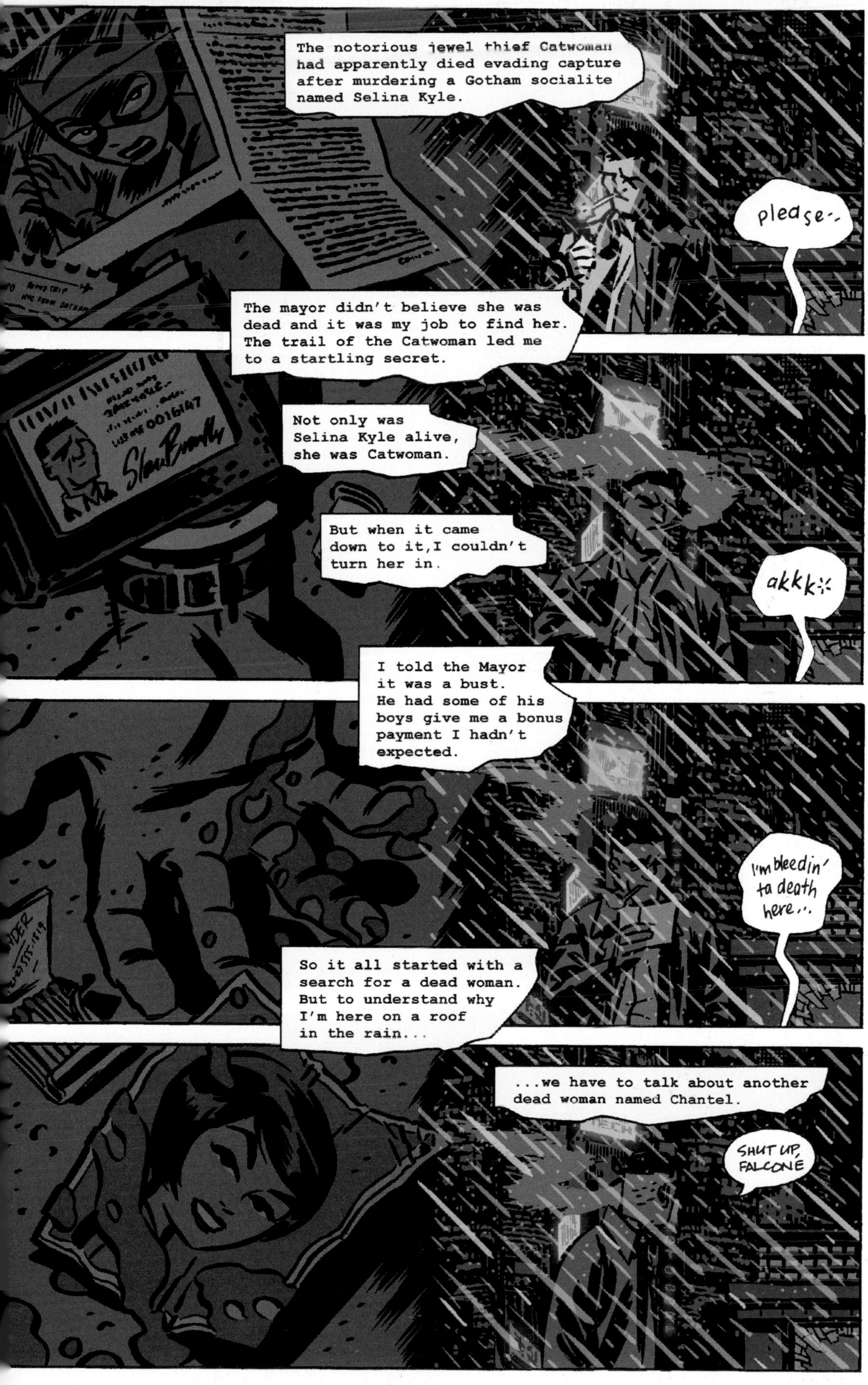
The notorious jewel thief Catwoman had apparently died evading capture after murdering a Gotham socialite named Selina Kyle.
please..
The mayor didn't believe she was dead and it was my job to find her. The trail of the Catwoman led me to a startling secret.
Not only was Selina Kyle alive, she was Catwoman.
But when it came down to it, I couldn't turn her in.
akkk
I told the Mayor it was a bust. He had some of his boys give me a bonus payment I hadn't expected.
I'm bleedin' ta death here...
So it all started with a search for a dead woman. But to understand why I'm here on a roof in the rain...
...we have to talk about another dead woman named Chantel.
SHUT UP, FALCONE

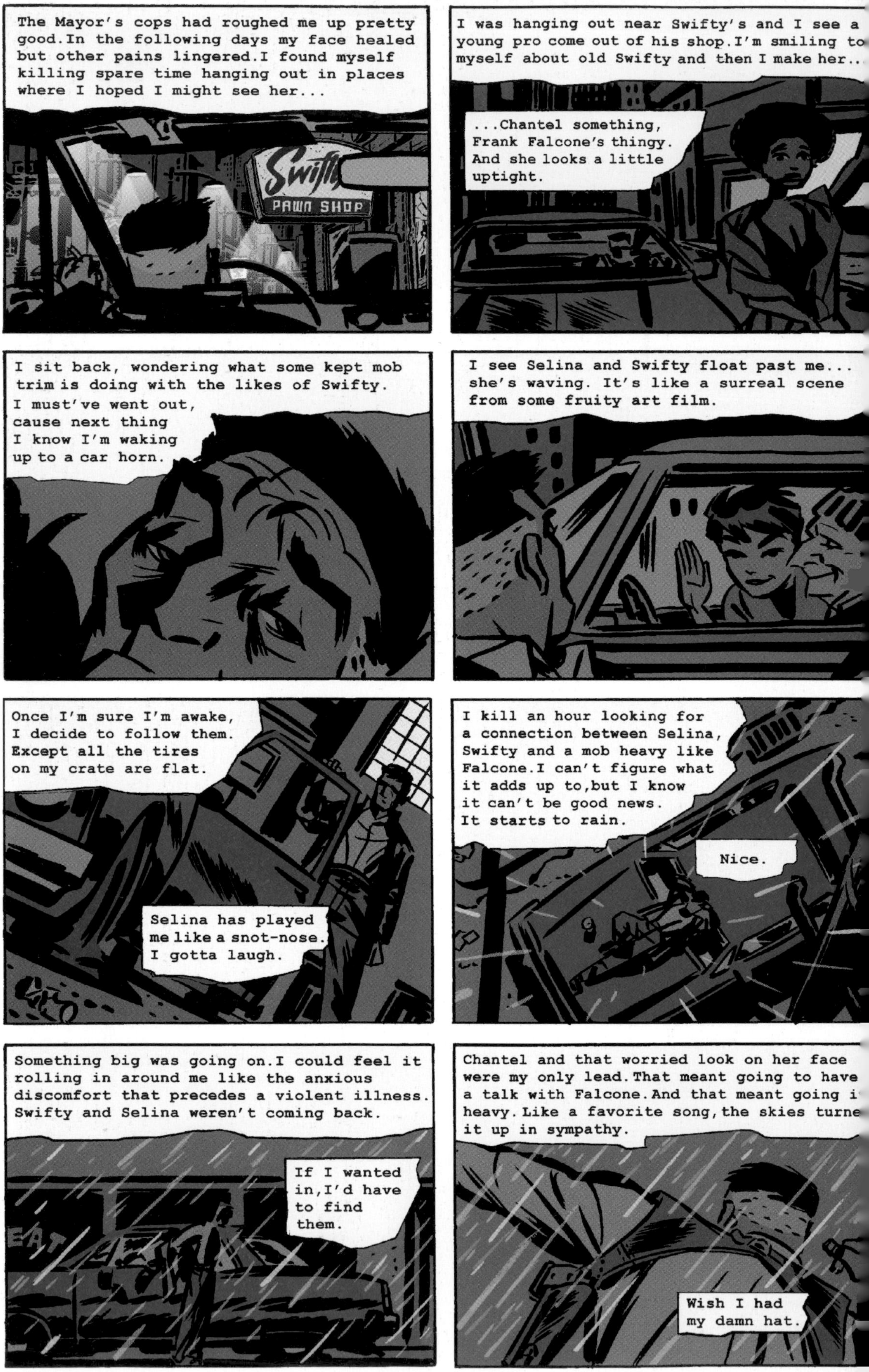

The Mayor's cops had roughed me up pretty good. In the following days my face healed but other pains lingered. I found myself killing spare time hanging out in places where I hoped I might see her...
Swifty
PAWN SHOP
I was hanging out near Swifty's and I see a young pro come out of his shop. I'm smiling to myself about old Swifty and then I make her...
...Chantel something, Frank Falcone's thingy. And she looks a little uptight.
I sit back, wondering what some kept mob trim is doing with the likes of Swifty.
I must've went out, cause next thing I know I'm waking up to a car horn.
I see Selina and Swifty float past me... she's waving. It's like a surreal scene from some fruity art film.
Once I'm sure I'm awake, I decide to follow them. Except all the tires on my crate are flat.
Selina has played me like a snot-nose. I gotta laugh.
I kill an hour looking for a connection between Selina, Swifty and a mob heavy like Falcone. I can't figure what it adds up to, but I know it can't be good news. It starts to rain.
Nice.
Something big was going on. I could feel it rolling in around me like the anxious discomfort that precedes a violent illness. Swifty and Selina weren't coming back.
If I wanted in, I'd have to find them.
Chantel and that worried look on her face were my only lead. That meant going to have a talk with Falcone. And that meant going i heavy. Like a favorite song, the skies turne it up in sympathy.
Wish I had my damn hat.

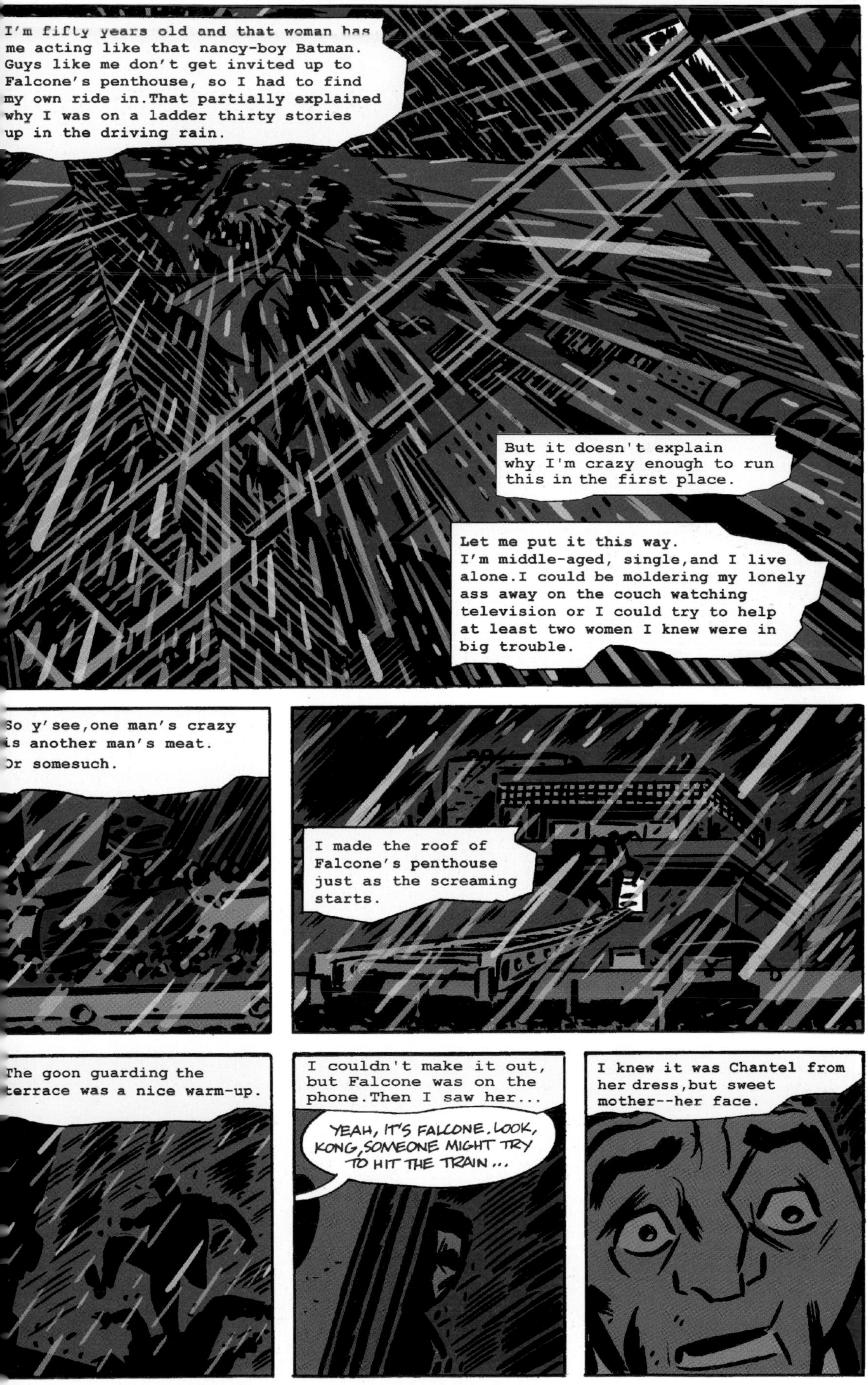
I'm fifty years old and that woman has me acting like that nancy-boy Batman. Guys like me don't get invited up to Falcone's penthouse, so I had to find my own ride in.That partially explained why I was on a ladder thirty stories up in the driving rain.
But it doesn't explain why I'm crazy enough to run this in the first place.
Let me put it this way. I'm middle-aged, single,and I live alone.I could be moldering my lonely ass away on the couch watching television or I could try to help at least two women I knew were in big trouble.
So y'see,one man's crazy is another man's meat. Or somesuch.
I made the roof of Falcone's penthouse just as the screaming starts.
The goon guarding the terrace was a nice warm-up.
I couldn't make it out, but Falcone was on the phone.Then I saw her...
YEAH, IT'S FALCONE. LOOK, KONG, SOMEONE MIGHT TRY TO HIT THE TRAIN...
I knew it was Chantel from her dress,but sweet mother--her face.

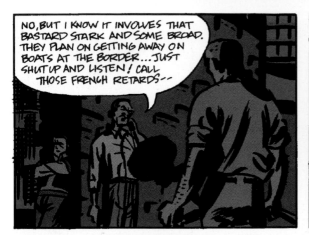
NO, BUT I KNOW IT INVOLVES THAT BASTARD STARK AND SOME BROAD. THEY PLAN ON GETTING AWAY ON BOATS AT THE BORDER...JUST SHUT UP AND LISTEN! CALL THOSE FRENCH RETARDS--

NO, THE OTHER ONE, LAPERIER. YOU TELL THAT FROG TO SEARCH THE RIVERFRONT FOR A CREW WITH A BOAT. YOU BOYS ON THE TRAIN GET READY FOR IT...

NO, GET BACK TO ME. I'M GONNA DEAL THIS TRAMP NOW.

My whole Irish life it's been the same. I need something to fight about. Something to fight for.

No fear, no doubt, no choice...

BAM

Just the righteous anger of the killer inside me.

BAM BAM BAM

BAM BAM

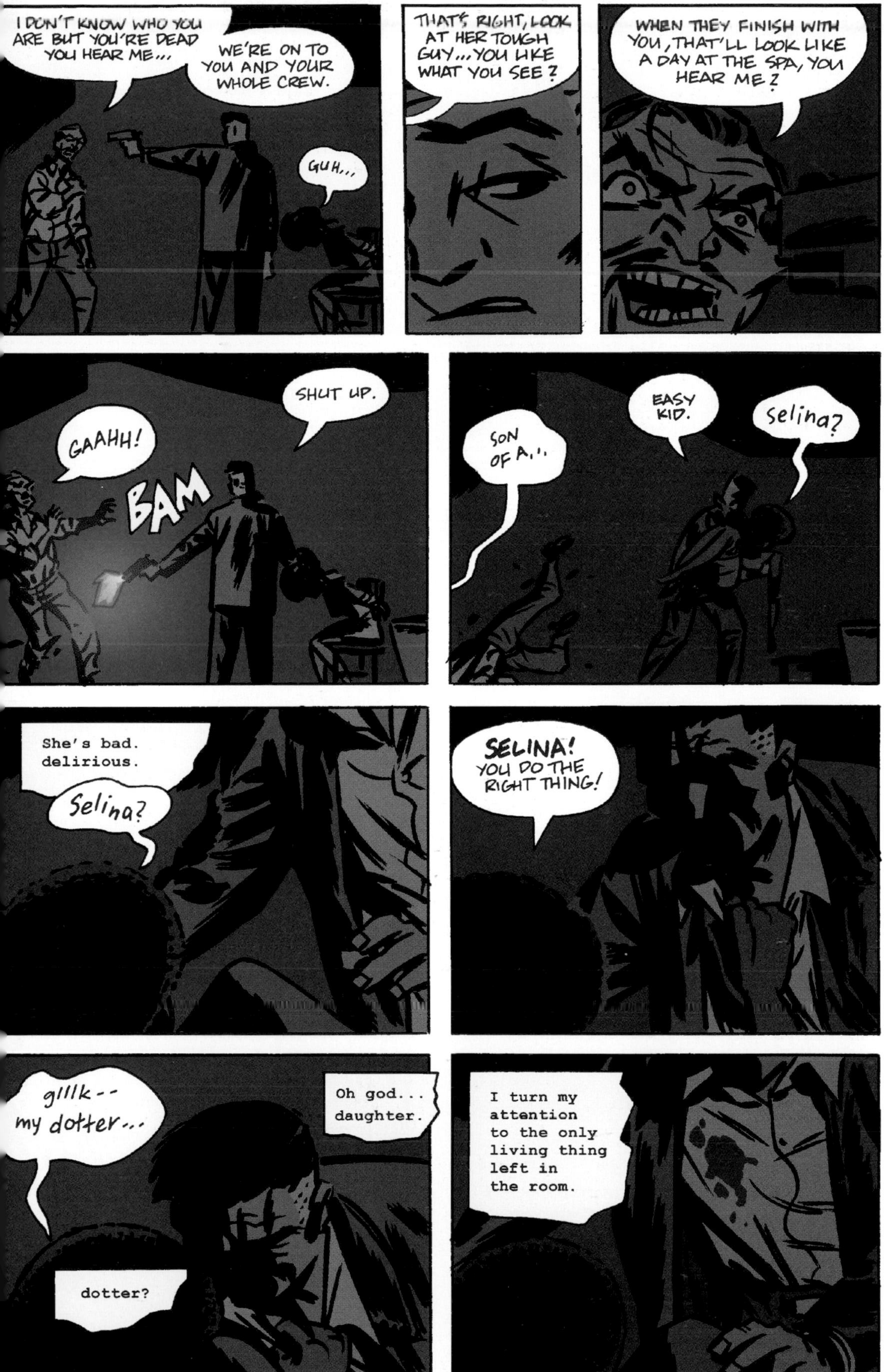
I DON'T KNOW WHO YOU ARE BUT YOU'RE DEAD YOU HEAR ME...
WE'RE ON TO YOU AND YOUR WHOLE CREW.
GUH...
THAT'S RIGHT, LOOK AT HER TOUGH GUY... YOU LIKE WHAT YOU SEE?
WHEN THEY FINISH WITH YOU, THAT'LL LOOK LIKE A DAY AT THE SPA, YOU HEAR ME?
SHUT UP.
GAAHH!
BAM
SON OF A...
EASY KID.
Selina?
She's bad. delirious.
Selina?
SELINA! YOU DO THE RIGHT THING!
glllk-- my dotter...
Oh god... daughter.
dotter?
I turn my attention to the only living thing left in the room.

Which, as they say, brings us up to speed.

THERE'S ONE MORE THING. YOU KEEP MENTIONING THIS MAN AND WOMAN WHO'RE TAKING DOWN YOUR TRAIN. I WANT NAMES.

HIS NAME'S STARK. *STARK!!* I DON'T KNOW THE GIRL'S NAME, I SWEAR! NOW PULL ME UP!! WE HAD A DEAL!

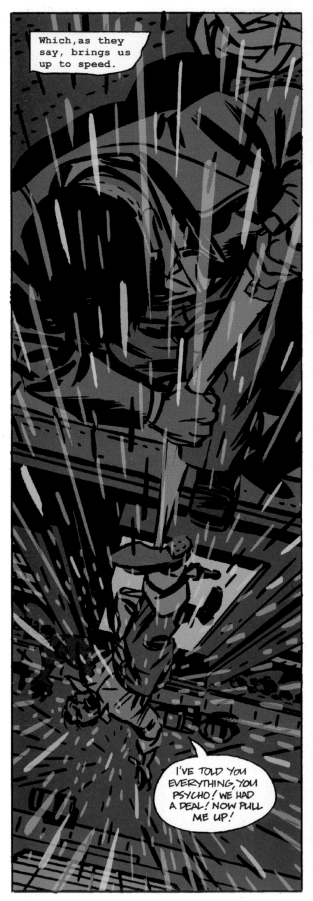

I'VE TOLD YOU EVERYTHING, YOU PSYCHO! WE HAD A DEAL! NOW PULL ME UP!

THE DEAL WAS I WOULDN'T KILL YOU. PULL YOURSELF UP.

NO!

I figure I'll take the stairs down. Should hustle. Cops'll be here soon.

CHANK

BASTARD.

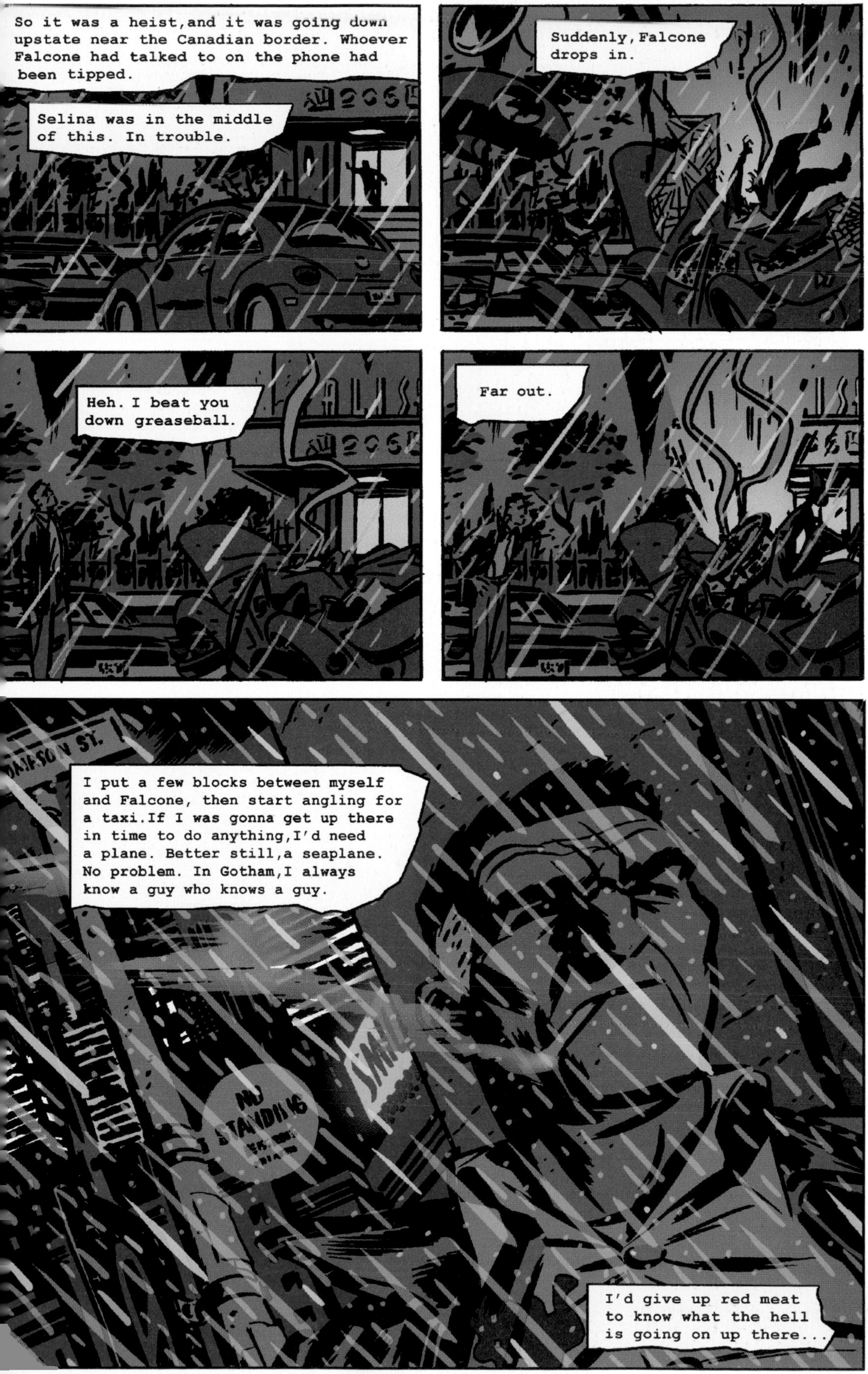
So it was a heist, and it was going down upstate near the Canadian border. Whoever Falcone had talked to on the phone had been tipped.
Selina was in the middle of this. In trouble.
Suddenly, Falcone drops in.
Heh. I beat you down greaseball.
Far out.
I put a few blocks between myself and Falcone, then start angling for a taxi. If I was gonna get up there in time to do anything, I'd need a plane. Better still, a seaplane. No problem. In Gotham, I always know a guy who knows a guy.
NO STANDING
I'd give up red meat to know what the hell is going on up there...

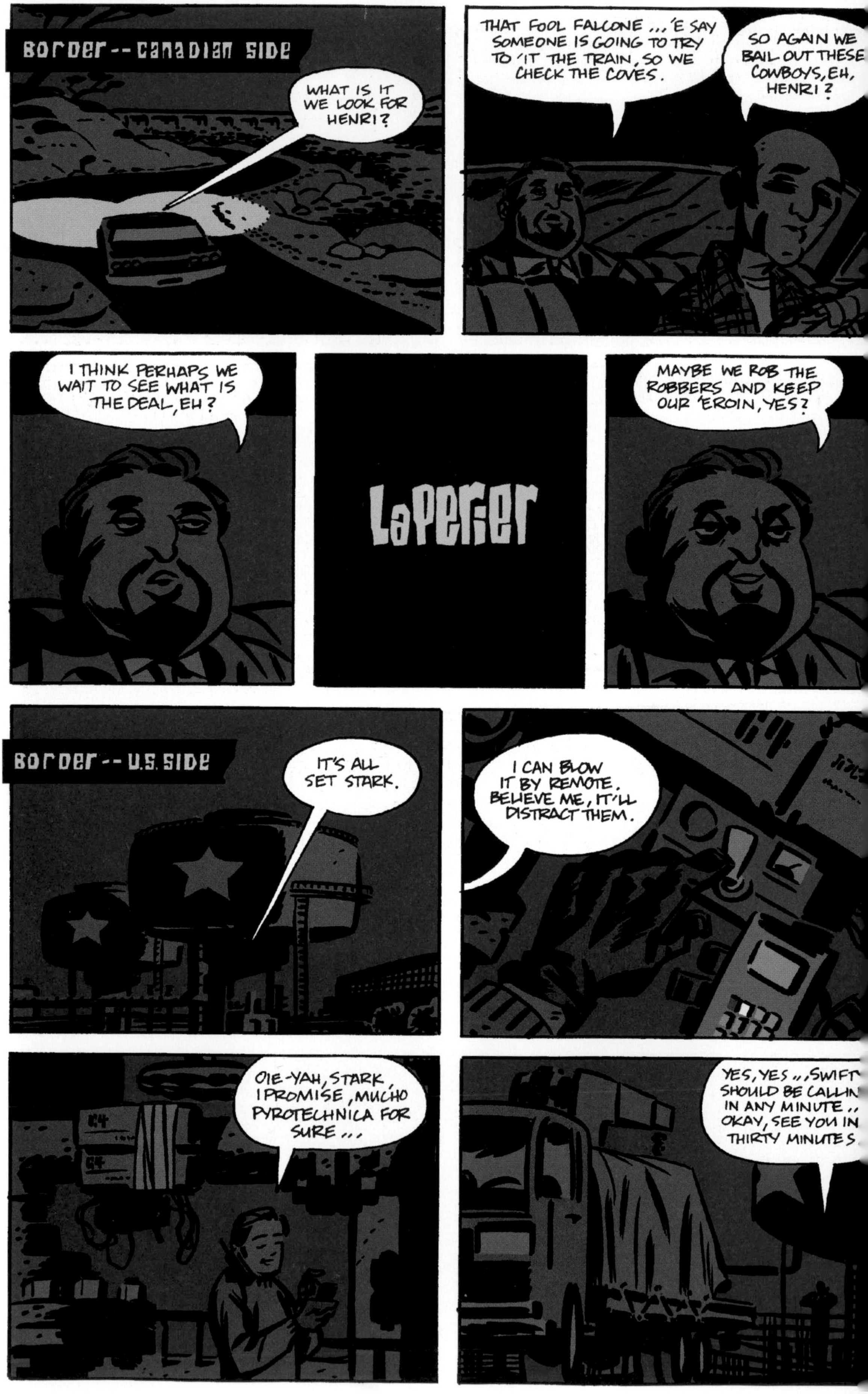
BORDER -- CANADIAN SIDE
WHAT IS IT WE LOOK FOR HENRI?
THAT FOOL FALCONE ..., 'E SAY SOMEONE IS GOING TO TRY TO 'IT THE TRAIN, SO WE CHECK THE COVES.
SO AGAIN WE BAIL OUT THESE COWBOYS, EH, HENRI?
I THINK PERHAPS WE WAIT TO SEE WHAT IS THE DEAL, EH?
LaPerier
MAYBE WE ROB THE ROBBERS AND KEEP OUR 'EROIN, YES?
BORDER -- U.S. SIDE
IT'S ALL SET STARK.
I CAN BLOW IT BY REMOTE. BELIEVE ME, IT'LL DISTRACT THEM.
OIE-YAH, STARK, I PROMISE, MUCHO PYROTECHNICA FOR SURE ...
YES, YES ..., SWIFT SHOULD BE CALLIN IN ANY MINUTE .. OKAY, SEE YOU IN THIRTY MINUTES.

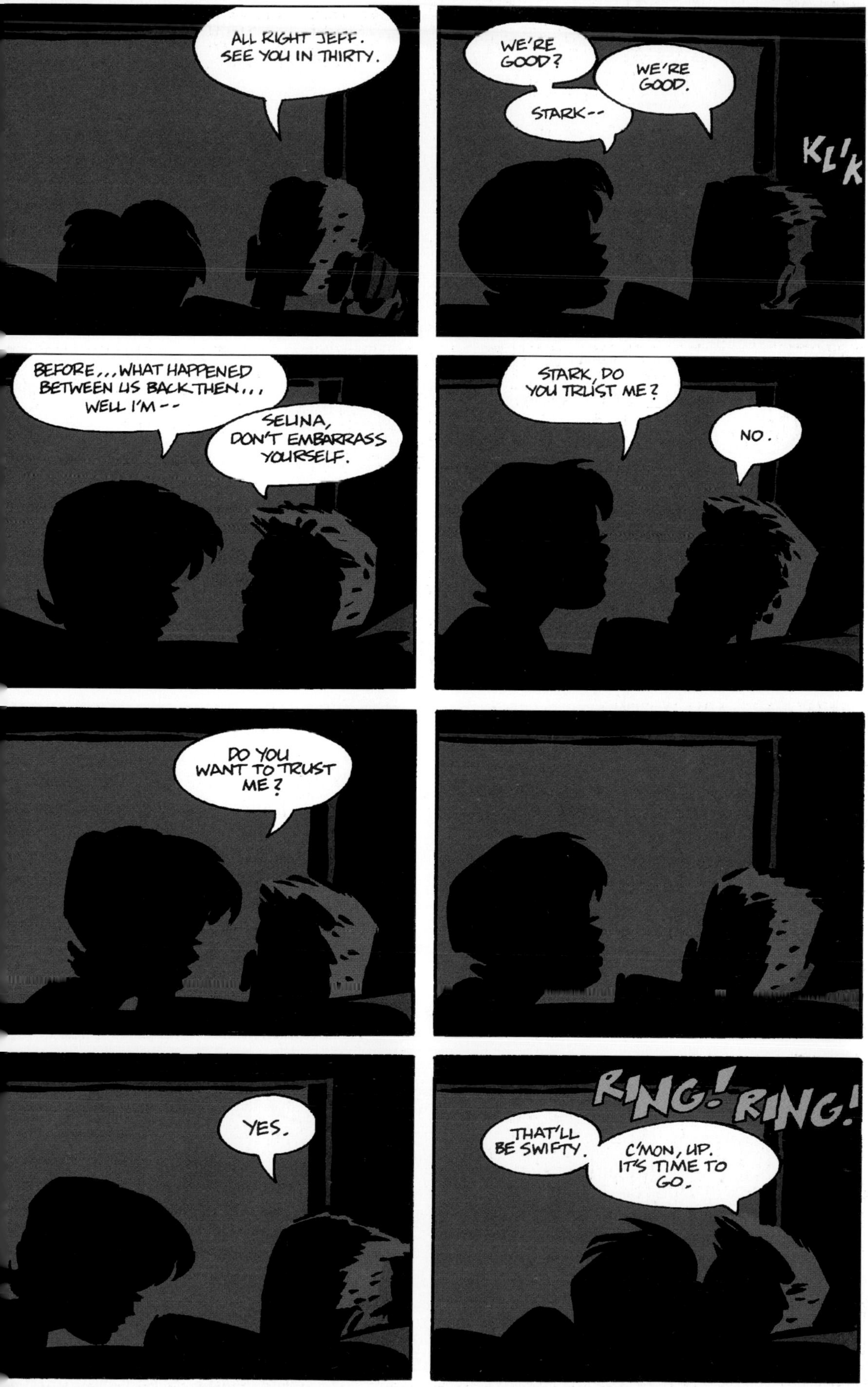
ALL RIGHT JEFF. SEE YOU IN THIRTY.
WE'RE GOOD?
WE'RE GOOD.
STARK--
KLIK
BEFORE... WHAT HAPPENED BETWEEN US BACK THEN... WELL I'M--
SELINA, DON'T EMBARRASS YOURSELF.
STARK, DO YOU TRUST ME?
NO.
DO YOU WANT TO TRUST ME?
YES.
RING! RING!
THAT'LL BE SWIFTY.
C'MON, UP. IT'S TIME TO GO.

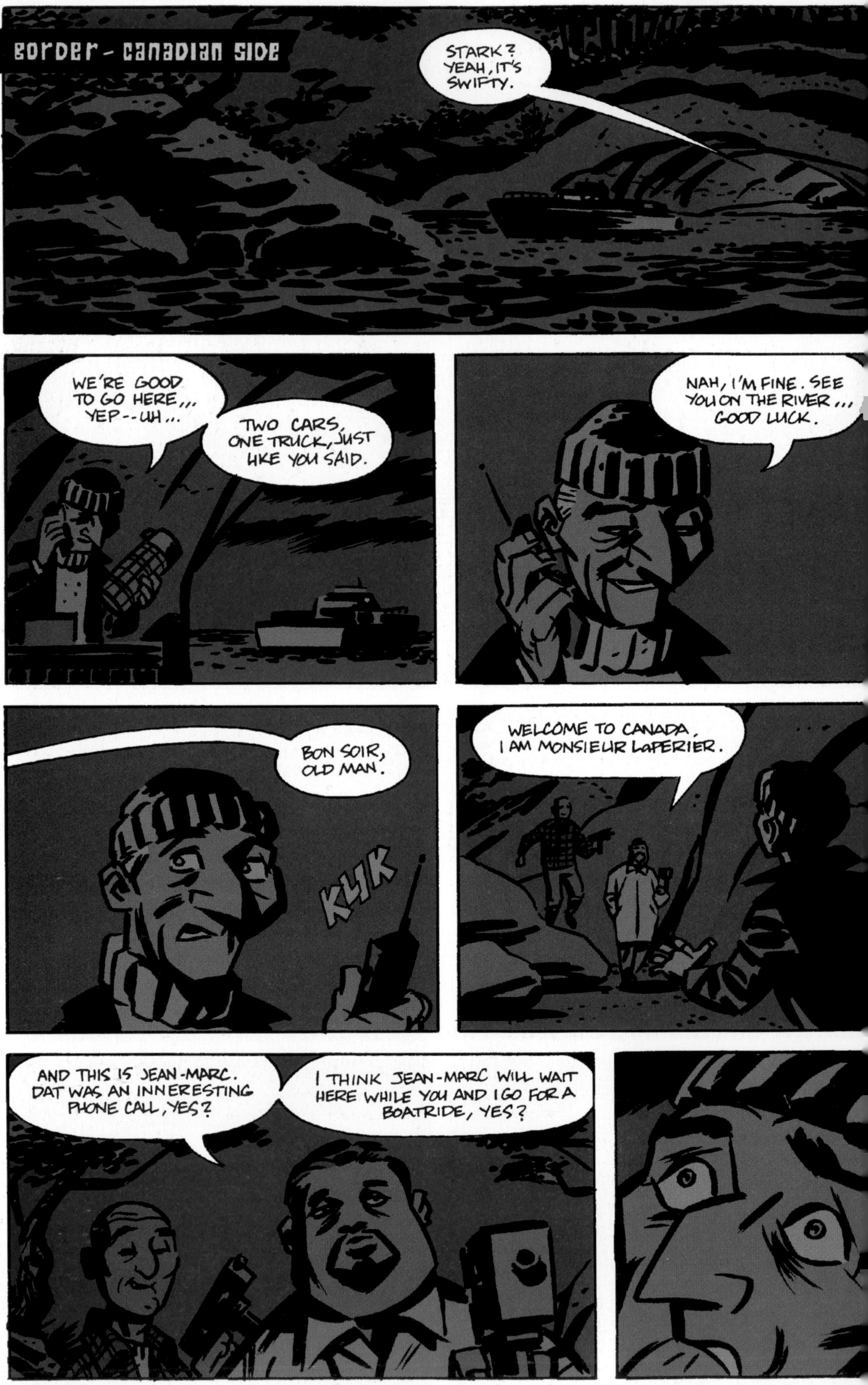
BORDER - CANADIAN SIDE
STARK? YEAH, IT'S SWIFTY.
WE'RE GOOD TO GO HERE,,, YEP--UH...
TWO CARS, ONE TRUCK, JUST LIKE YOU SAID.
NAH, I'M FINE. SEE YOU ON THE RIVER,,, GOOD LUCK.
BON SOIR, OLD MAN.
KLIK
WELCOME TO CANADA, I AM MONSIEUR LaPERIER.
AND THIS IS JEAN-MARC. DAT WAS AN INNERESTING PHONE CALL, YES?
I THINK JEAN-MARC WILL WAIT HERE WHILE YOU AND I GO FOR A BOATRIDE, YES?

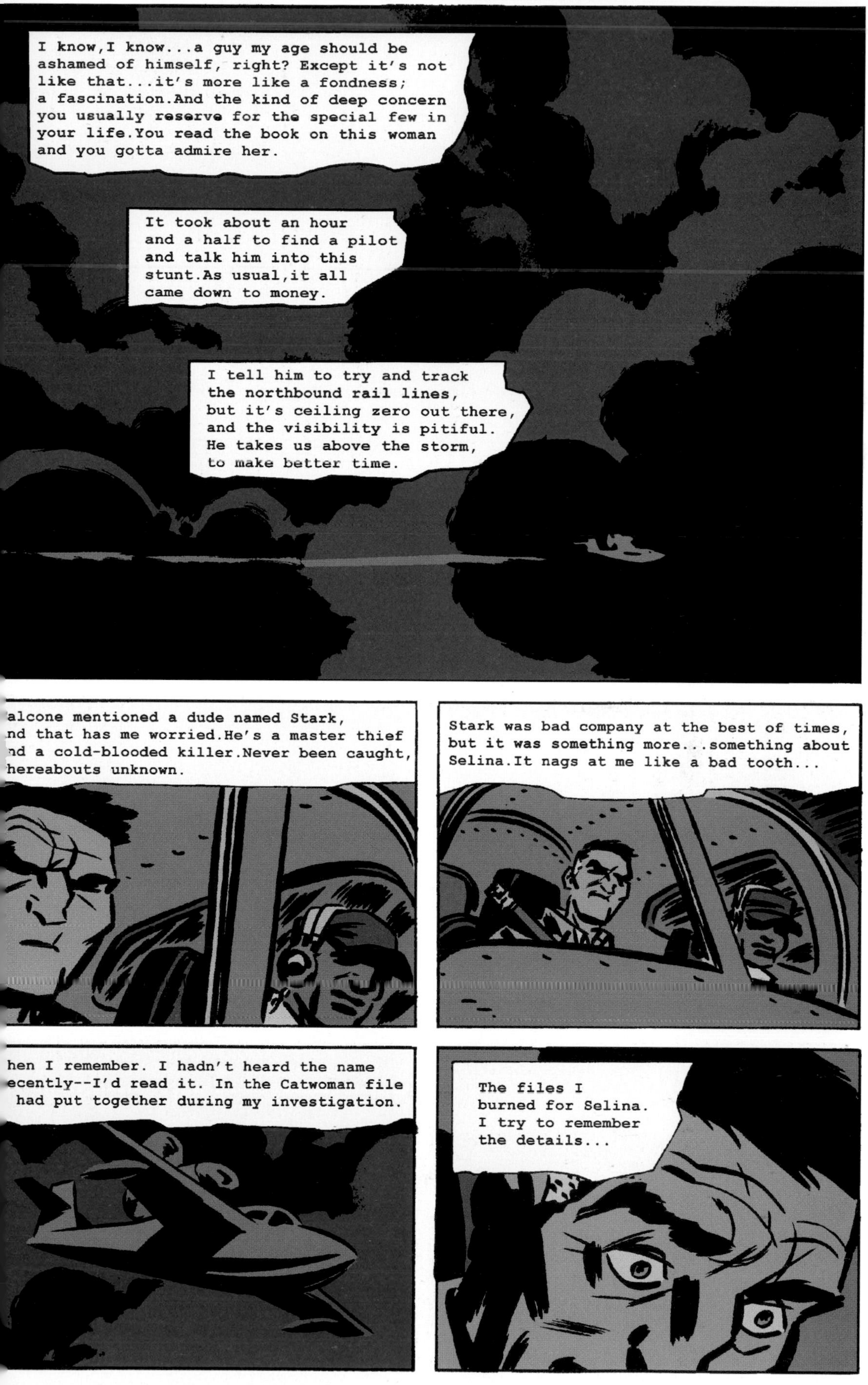
I know,I know...a guy my age should be ashamed of himself, right? Except it's not like that...it's more like a fondness; a fascination.And the kind of deep concern you usually reserve for the special few in your life.You read the book on this woman and you gotta admire her.
It took about an hour and a half to find a pilot and talk him into this stunt.As usual,it all came down to money.
I tell him to try and track the northbound rail lines, but it's ceiling zero out there, and the visibility is pitiful. He takes us above the storm, to make better time.
alcone mentioned a dude named Stark, nd that has me worried.He's a master thief nd a cold-blooded killer.Never been caught, hereabouts unknown.
Stark was bad company at the best of times, but it was something more...something about Selina.It nags at me like a bad tooth...
hen I remember. I hadn't heard the name ecently--I'd read it. In the Catwoman file had put together during my investigation.
The files I burned for Selina. I try to remember the details...

...it was a diamond robbery. Stark and an associate named "Fingers" Marotta took down a Falcone courier for about half a million in uncut stones.

But something went wrong.

There was a hell of a firefight and "Fingers" was hit. Stark apparently didn't bat an eye.

He picked up that bag and made for the street in a hail of bullets.

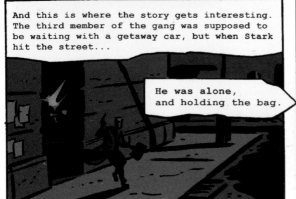

And this is where the story gets interesting. The third member of the gang was supposed to be waiting with a getaway car, but when Stark hit the street...

He was alone, and holding the bag.

This part was told to the cops by an eyewitness. A homeless shmoe or somesuch...A whip snaked down out of the night, plucking the diamonds from Stark's hand.

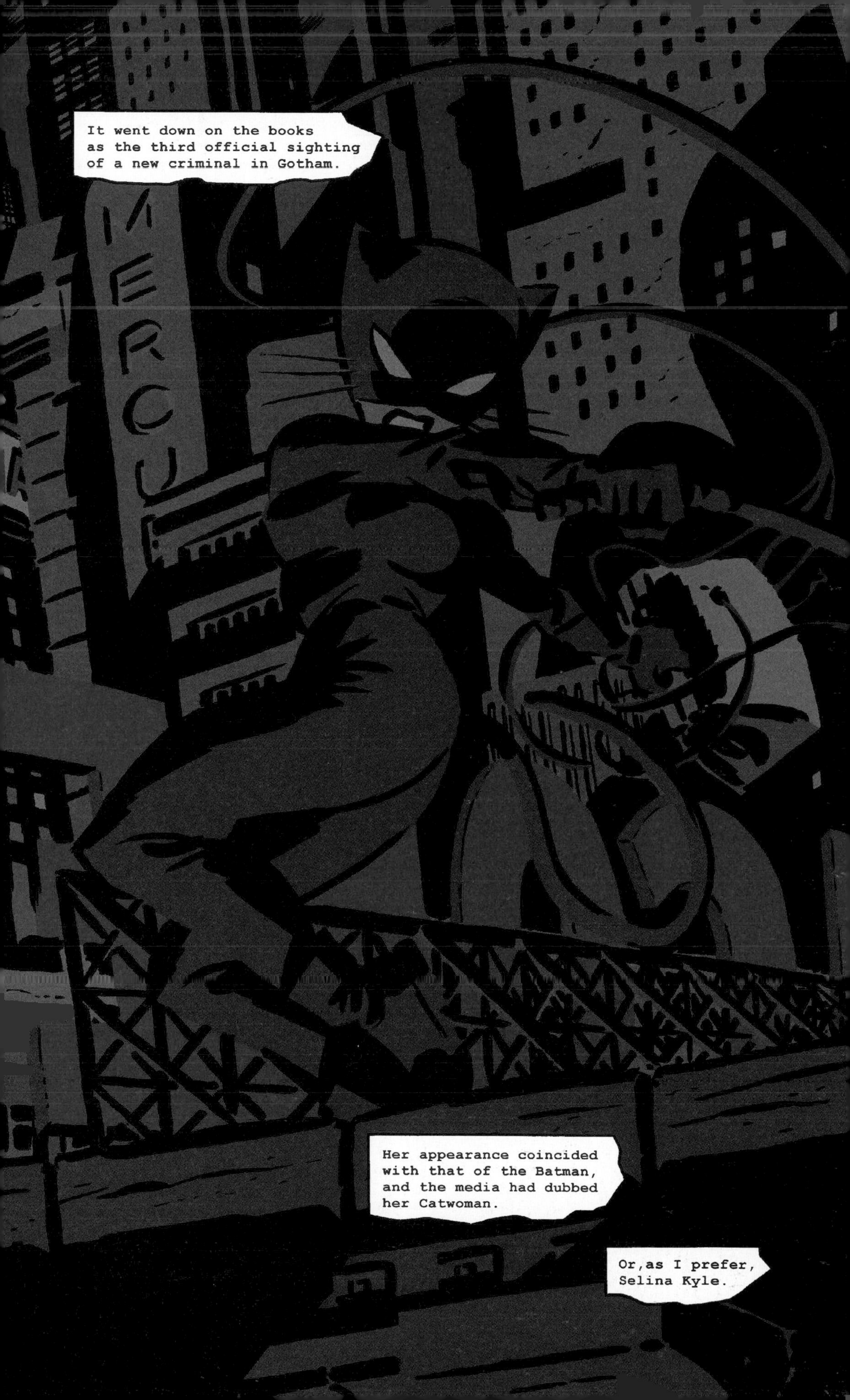
It went down on the books as the third official sighting of a new criminal in Gotham.
Her appearance coincided with that of the Batman, and the media had dubbed her Catwoman.
Or, as I prefer, Selina Kyle.

It's hard to imagine what went through Stark's mind. Did he know who was behind the mask?

What happened to the driver of the getaway car?

According to the witness, Stark just stood there without firing a shot, as the sound of a cracking whip took her away into the night.

The boys got hold of "Fingers" before he checked out. He gave up Stark and "some girl" before he died on them.

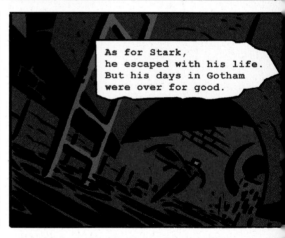

As for Stark, he escaped with his life. But his days in Gotham were over for good.

The clouds pull open in front of us and below us is the border. We've flown clear of the storm.

Tonight I killed three men and held a twenty-year-old girl in my arms while she died. But God help me, it felt like the worst was yet to come.

66

Book Four

score

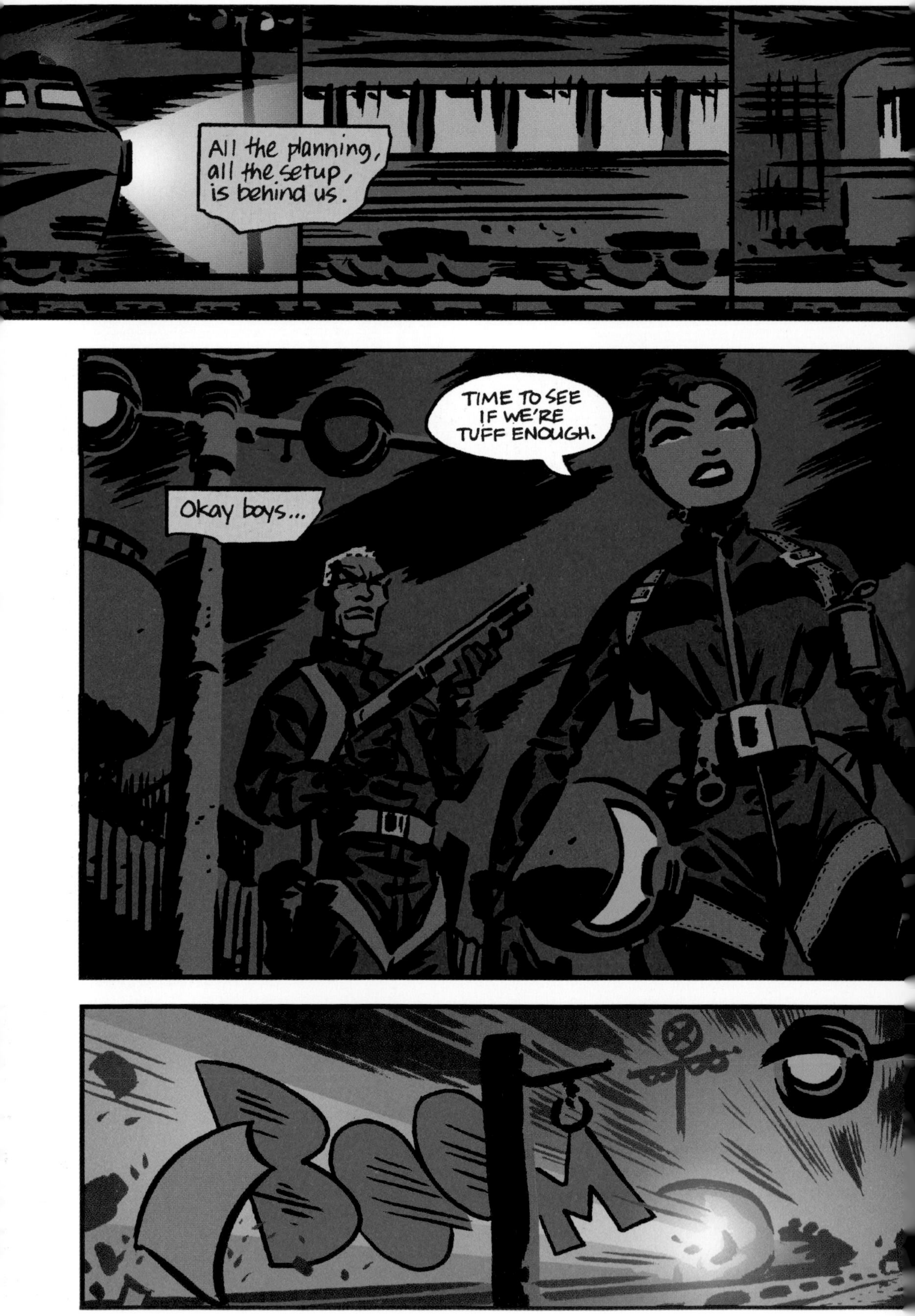
All the planning, all the setup, is behind us.
Okay boys...
TIME TO SEE IF WE'RE TUFF ENOUGH.
BOOM

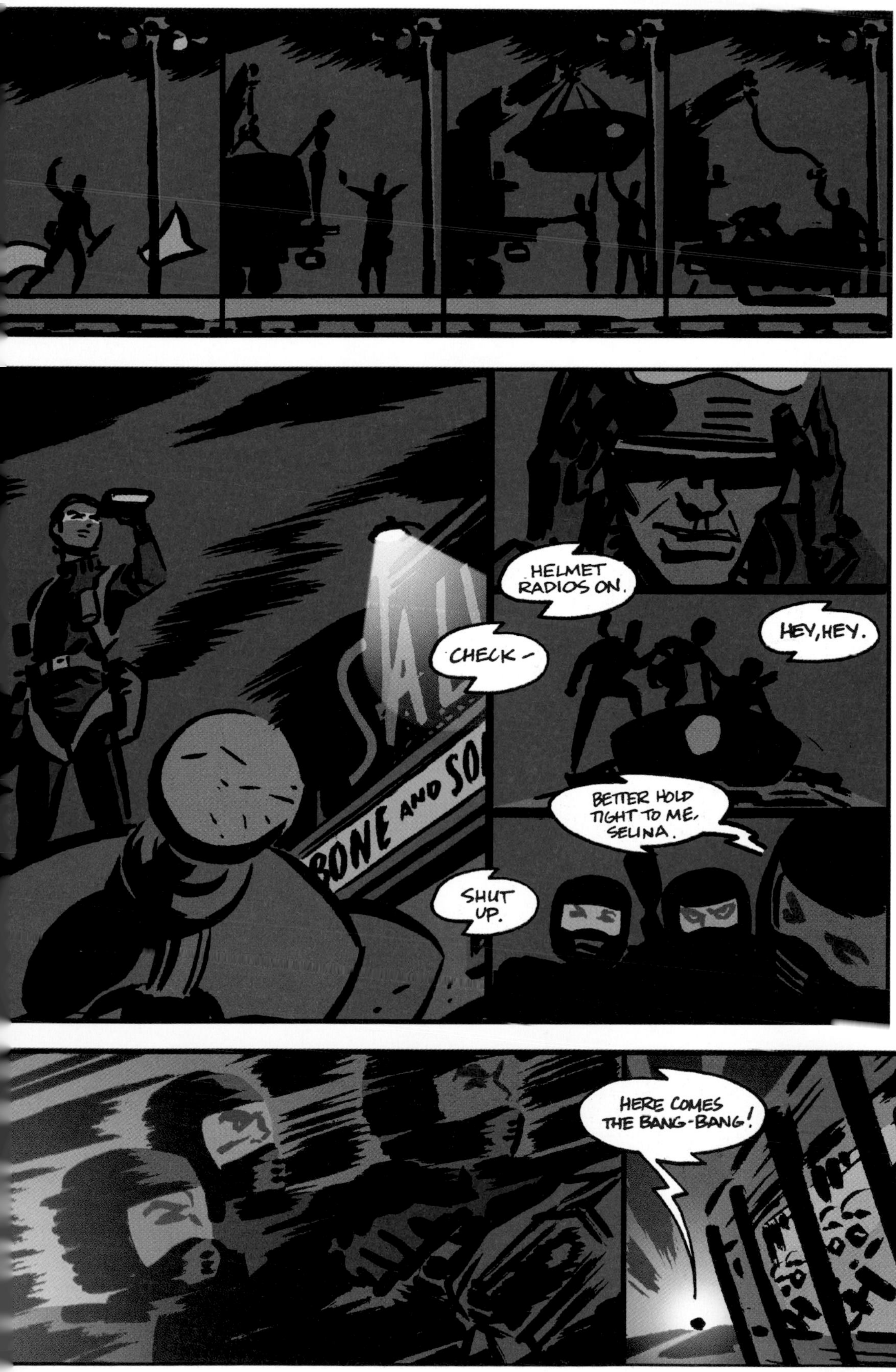
HELMET RADIOS ON.
CHECK -
HEY, HEY.
BETTER HOLD TIGHT TO ME, SELINA.
SHUT UP.
BONE AND SO
HERE COMES THE BANG-BANG!

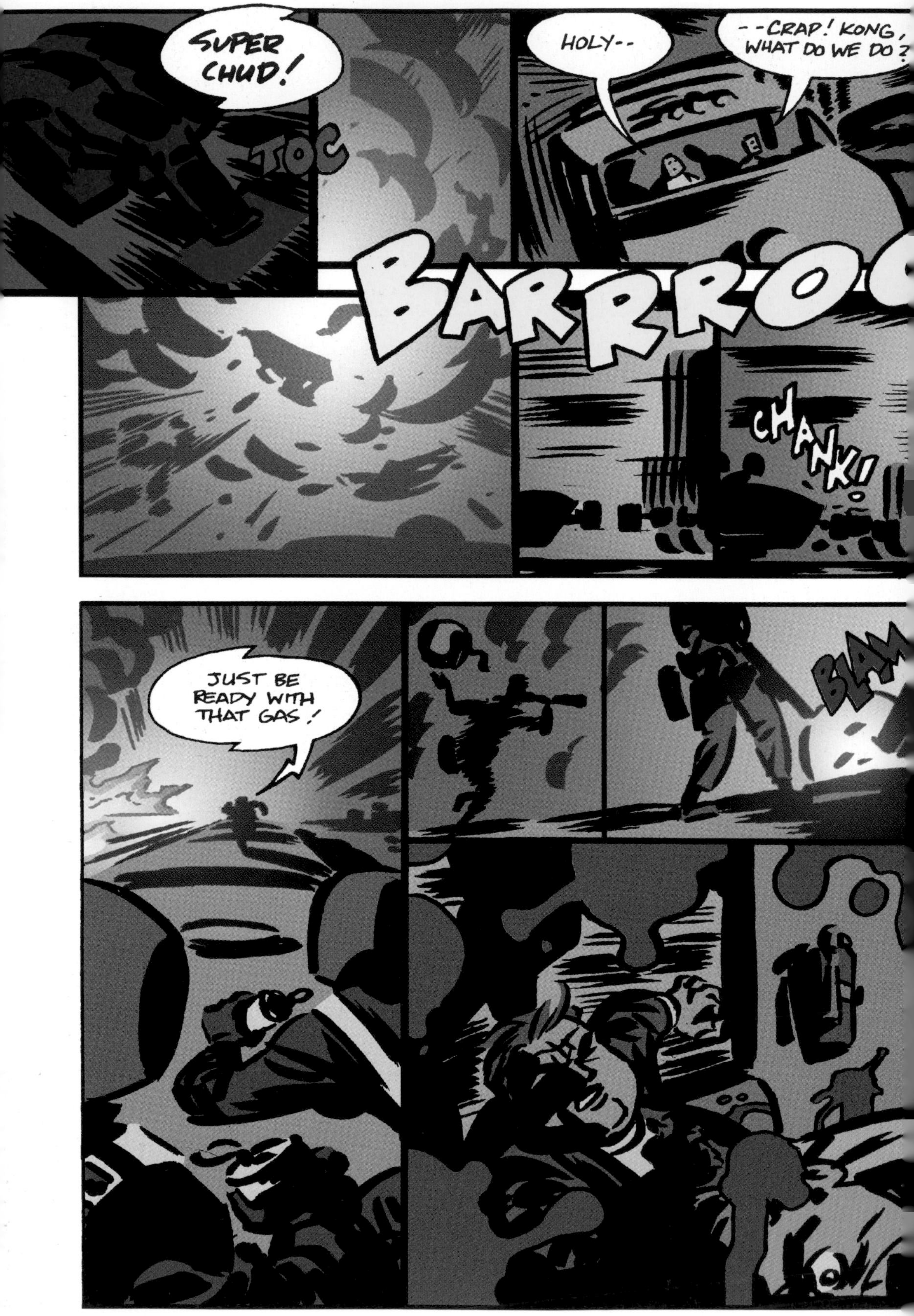

SUPER CHUD!
TOC
HOLY--
--CRAP! KONG, WHAT DO WE DO?
BARROO
CHANK!
JUST BE READY WITH THAT GAS!
BLAM

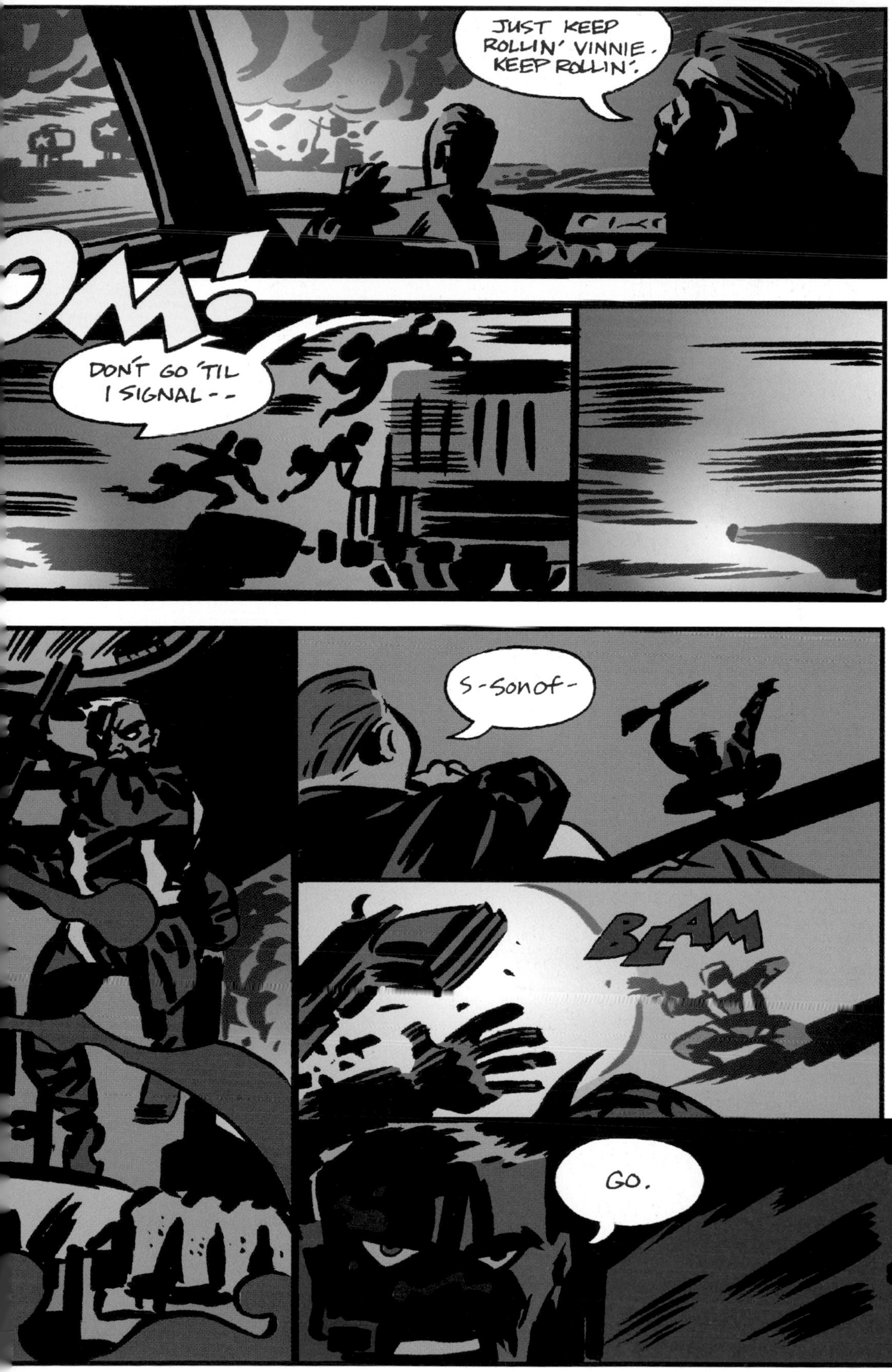
JUST KEEP ROLLIN' VINNIE. KEEP ROLLIN'.
OOM!
DON'T GO 'TIL I SIGNAL--
S-SONOF-
BLAM
GO.

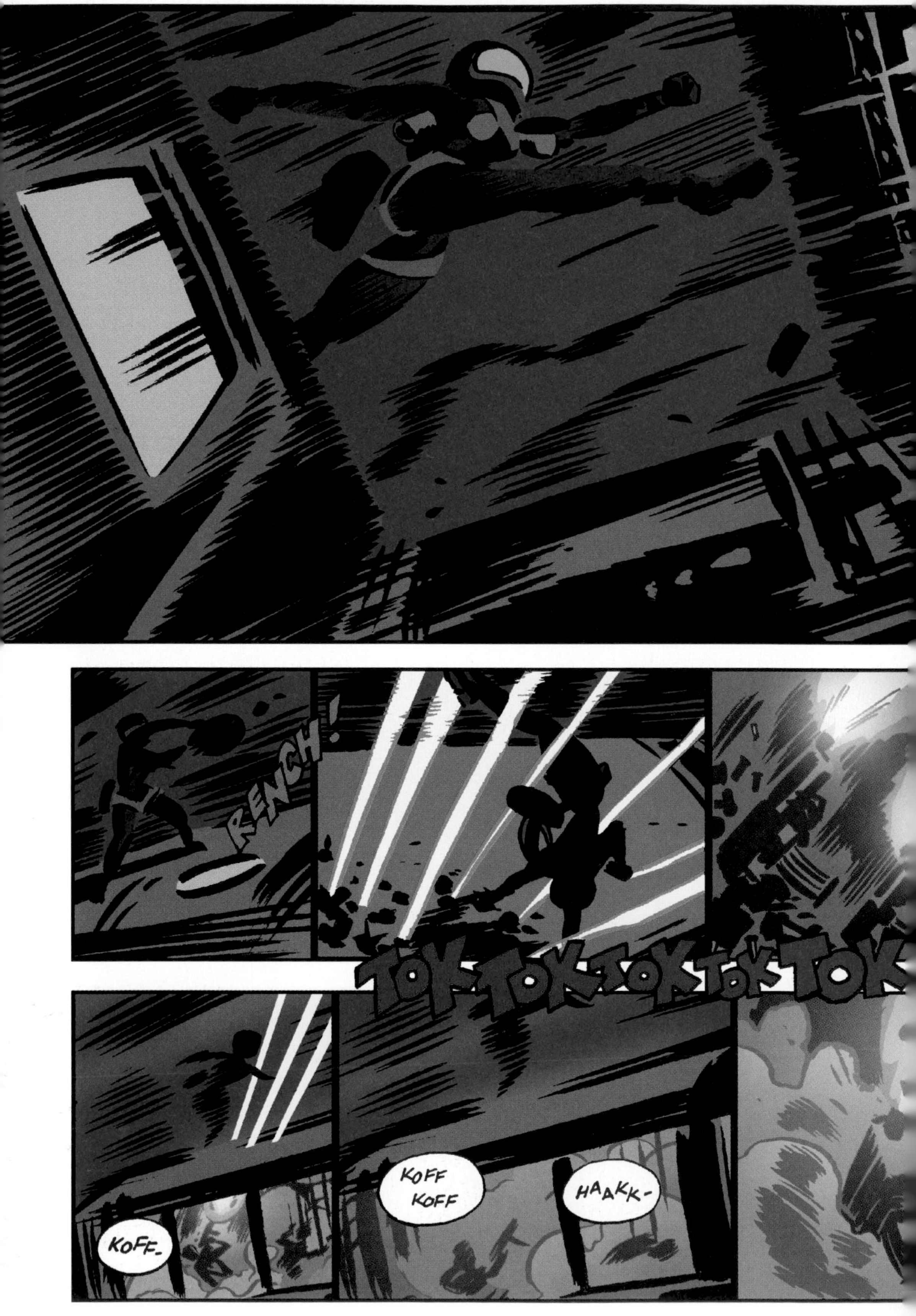
RENCH!
TOK TOK TOK TOK TOK
KOFF-
KOFF KOFF
HAAKK-

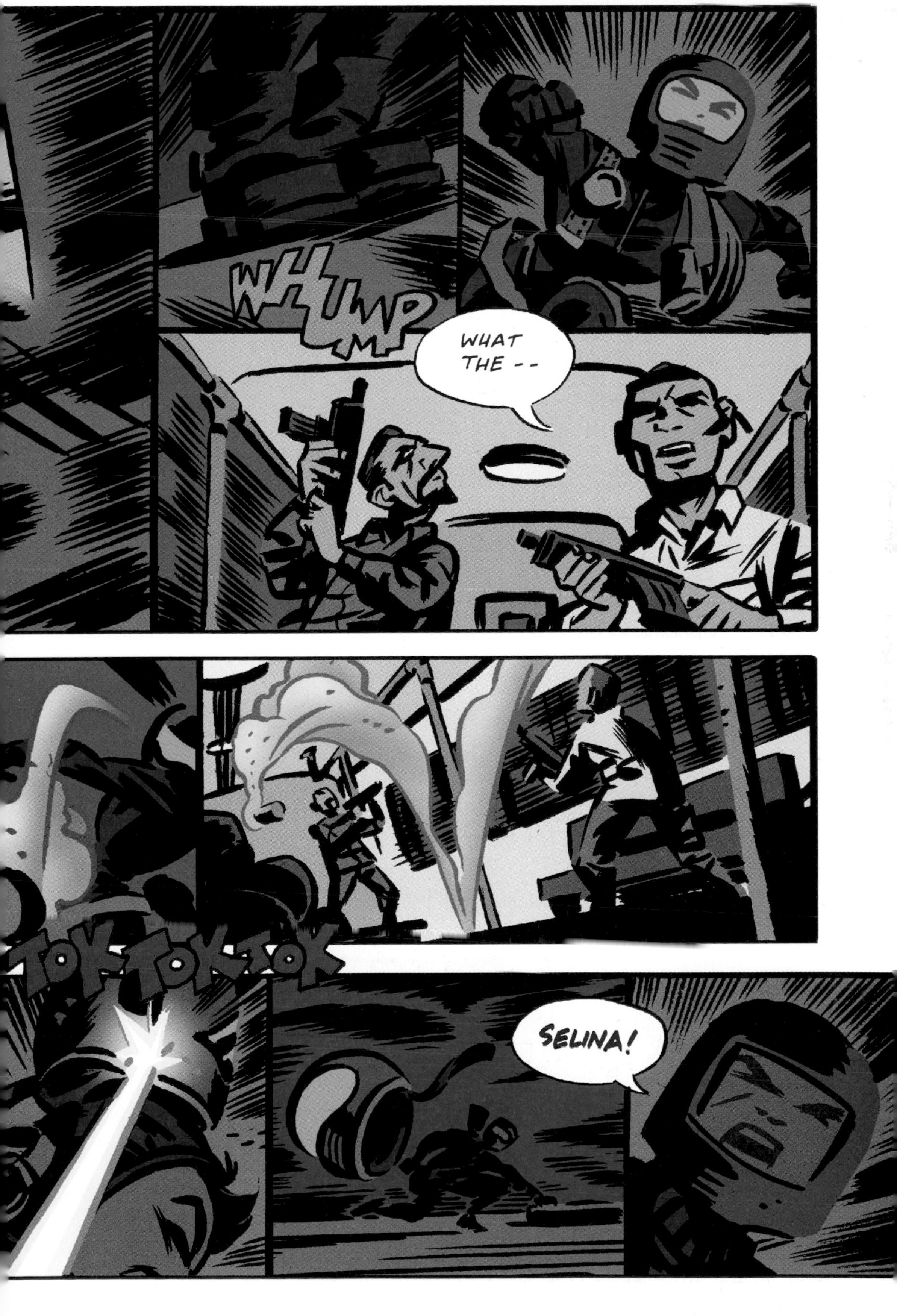
WHUMP
WHAT THE --
TOK TOK TOK
SELINA!

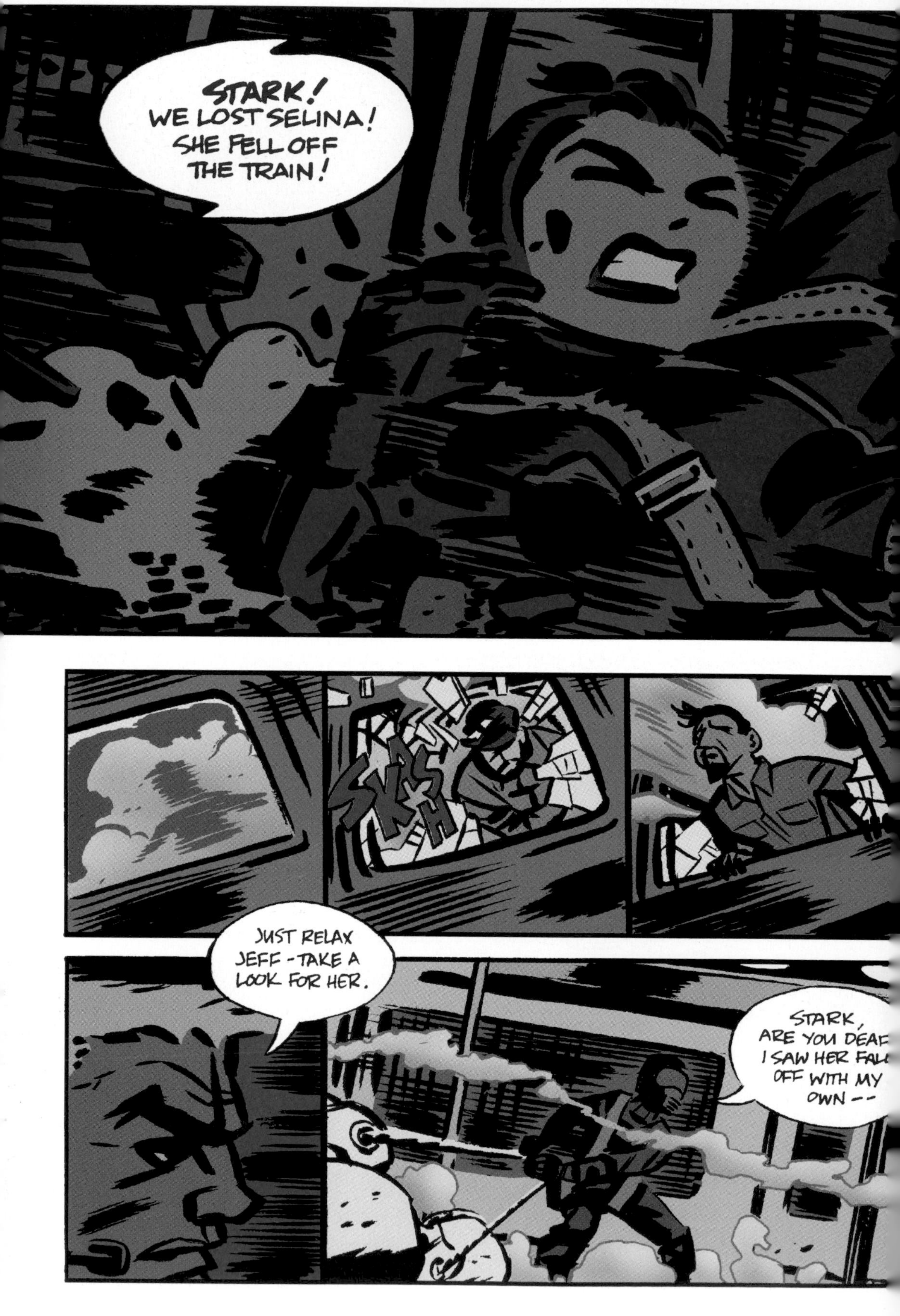
STARK!
WE LOST SELINA!
SHE FELL OFF
THE TRAIN!
SKRASH
JUST RELAX
JEFF - TAKE A
LOOK FOR HER.
STARK,
ARE YOU DEAF
I SAW HER FALL
OFF WITH MY
OWN --

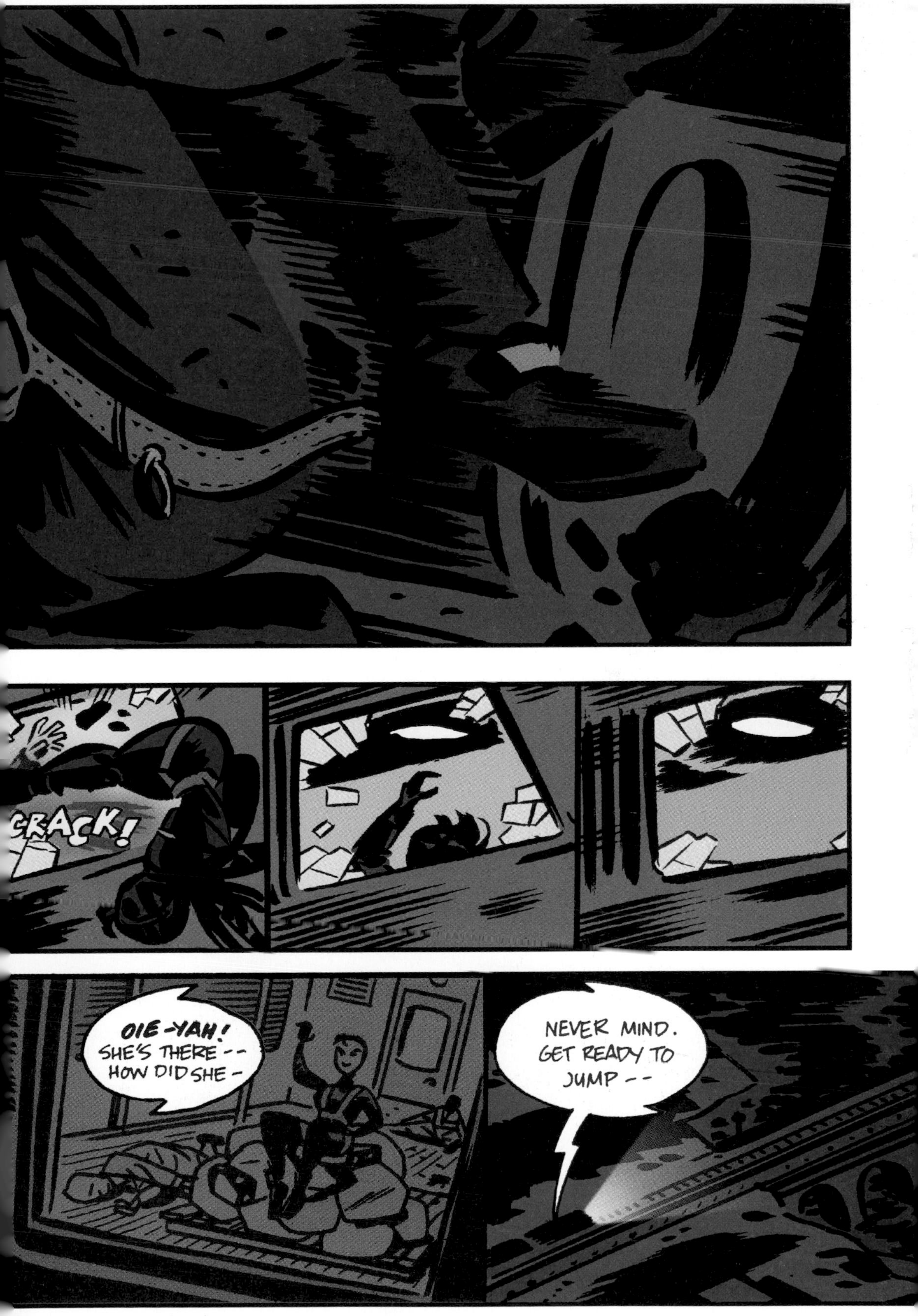
CRACK!
OIE-YAH! SHE'S THERE -- HOW DID SHE -
NEVER MIND. GET READY TO JUMP --

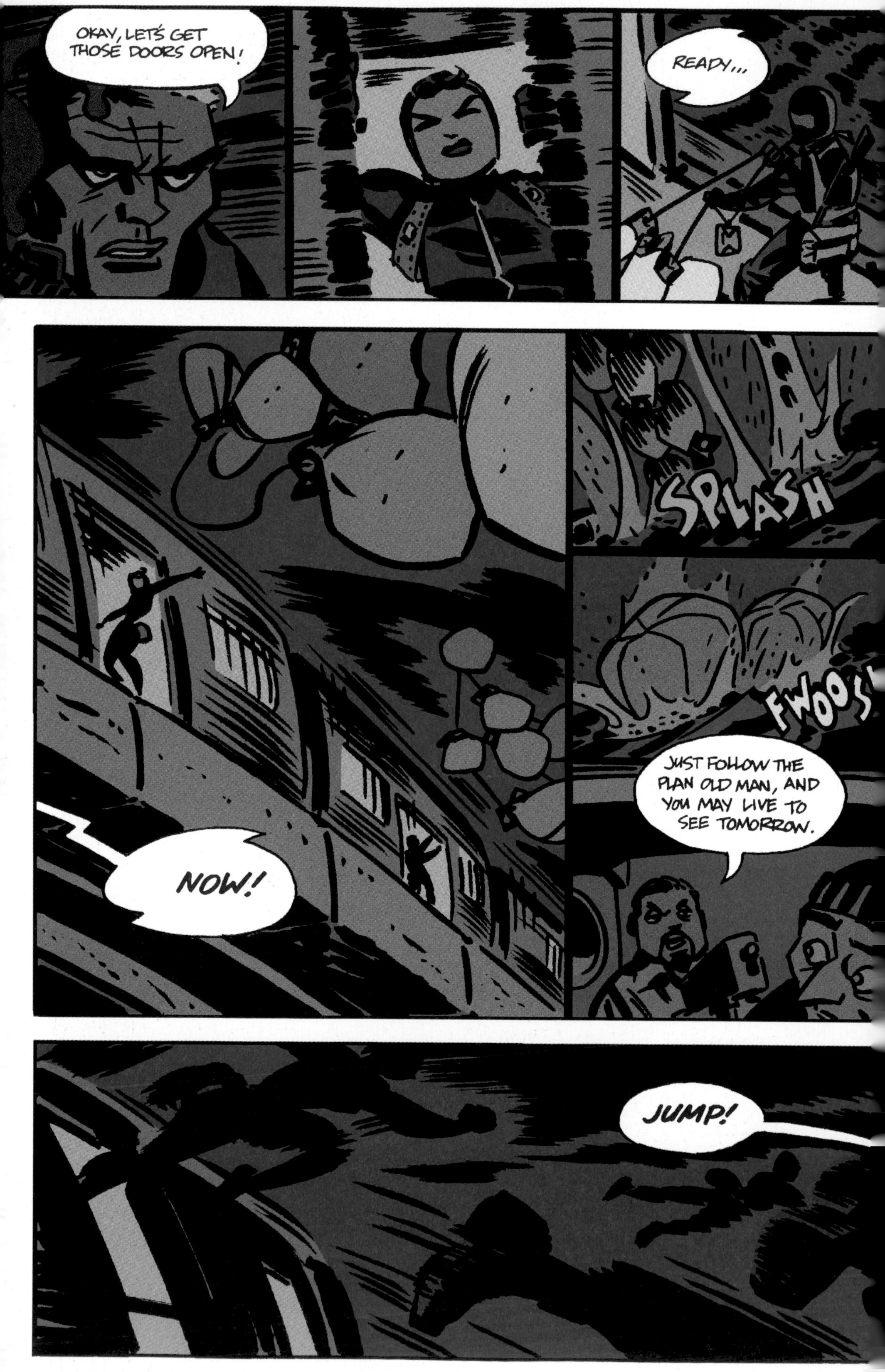
OKAY, LET'S GET THOSE DOORS OPEN!
READY...
SPLASH
FWOOS
JUST FOLLOW THE PLAN OLD MAN, AND YOU MAY LIVE TO SEE TOMORROW.
NOW!
JUMP!

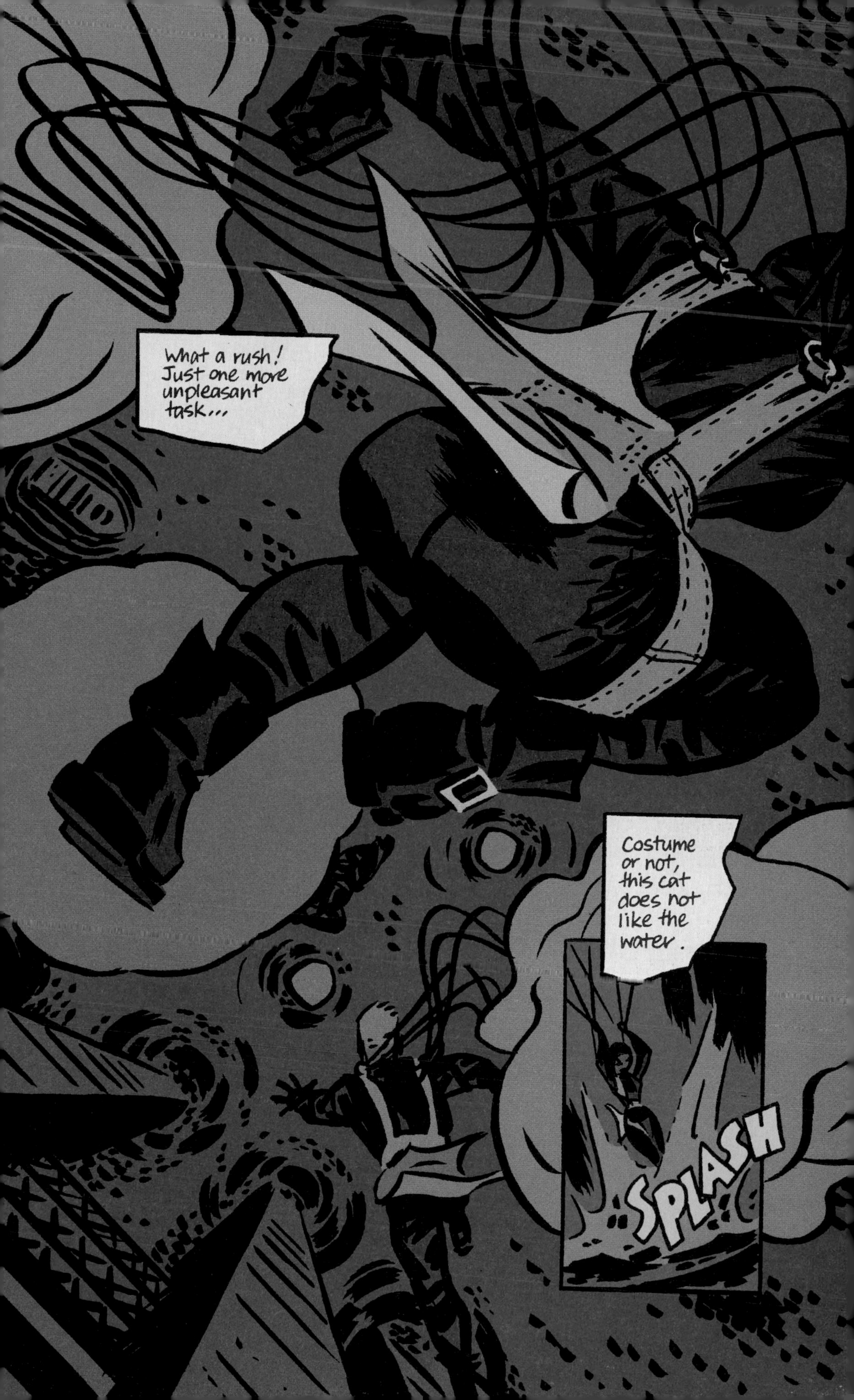
What a rush! Just one more unpleasant task...
Costume or not, this cat does not like the water.
SPLASH

I swim towards the dim outline of the floats. The boat slowly grows in the darkness...

It's quite clever really... the moneybags go into a net, underneath the surface. No loading, no evidence onboard.

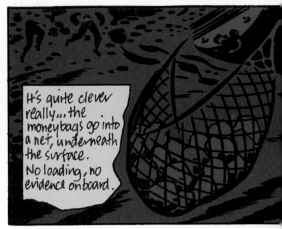

For a moment I'm consumed by the childish fear that something horrible will rise from the depths and snatch me away... But Stark is the only predator in this water— and he's my predator.

SELINA! IS THAT YOU!

WELL, IT ISN'T ANGIE DICKINSON.

OIE-YAH! THERE SHE IS! I THOUGHT MAYBE YOU DROWN, HEY?

AND LET YOU CLAIM MY SHARE? FAT CHANCE PRETTY BOY.

SO NOW THAT I'M A MILLIONAIRE, MAYBE YOU BE MY DATE, HUH?

SORRY JEFF. I LIKE 'EM RICH AND TOO OLD TO RUN AWAY.

HRMF.

I TOLD YOU STARK, SELINA IS OUR LUCKY GIRL, HEY?

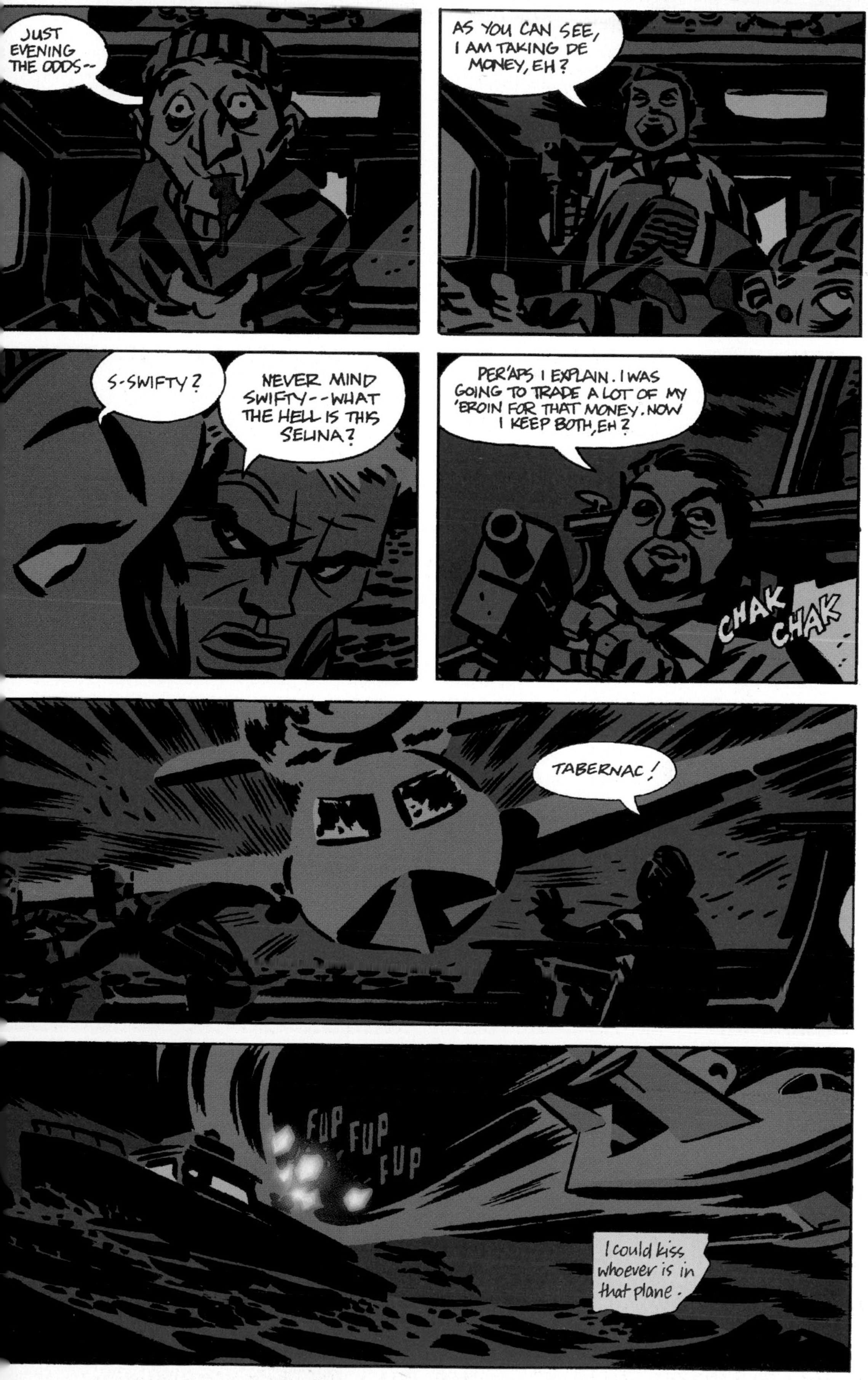
JUST EVENING THE ODDS--
AS YOU CAN SEE, I AM TAKING DE MONEY, EH?
S-SWIFTY?
NEVER MIND SWIFTY--WHAT THE HELL IS THIS SELINA?
PER'APS I EXPLAIN. I WAS GOING TO TRADE A LOT OF MY 'EROIN FOR THAT MONEY. NOW I KEEP BOTH, EH?
CHAK CHAK
TABERNAC!
FUP FUP FUP
I could kiss whoever is in that plane.

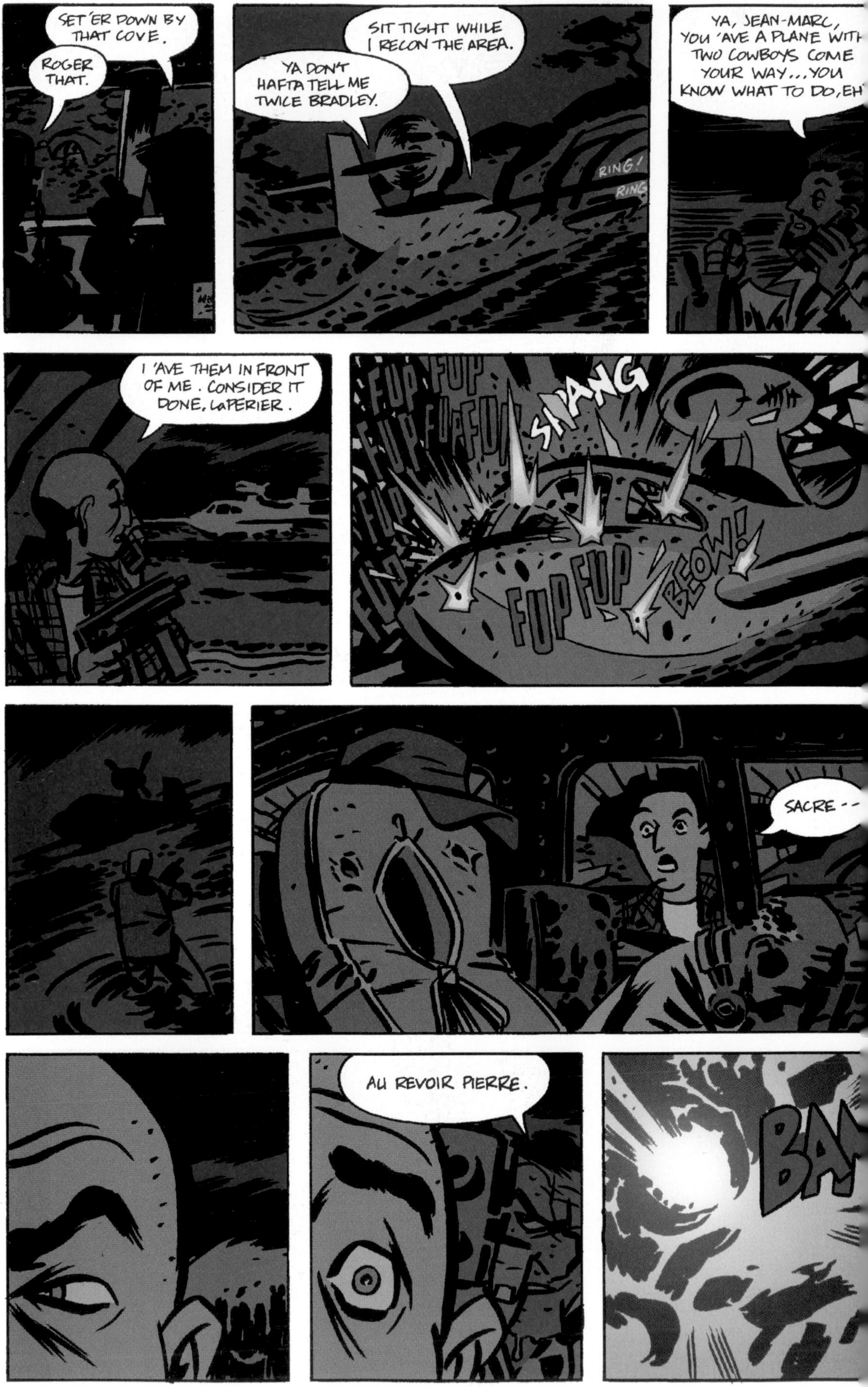

SET 'ER DOWN BY THAT COVE.
ROGER THAT.
SIT TIGHT WHILE I RECON THE AREA.
YA DON'T HAFTA TELL ME TWICE BRADLEY.
RING! RING
YA, JEAN-MARC, YOU 'AVE A PLANE WITH TWO COWBOYS COME YOUR WAY... YOU KNOW WHAT TO DO, EH
I 'AVE THEM IN FRONT OF ME. CONSIDER IT DONE, LaPERIER.
FUP FUP FUP FUFUP
SPANG
FUP FUP
BEOW!
SACRE --
AU REVOIR PIERRE.

There's a moment when you discover the truth about how someone feels about you.

After we hit the water, the Frenchman bolted.

You see, Stark had a hold of the net when the boat got underway. He could've left me there, but he didn't ... He took my hand.

We'd see it to the end together.

Frenchie's machine gun rules out the direct approach. Stark forms a quick plan—

I figure get rid of him and be done with it, but Stark wants to know who this clown works for. We do it his way.

HEY!!

I hope Frenchie likes girls.

WELL NOW, WHAT 'AVE WE HERE - YOU MUST 'AVE NINE LIVES, CHERE.

CATS HAVE NINE LIVES, BUT LAST I HEARD, FROGS ONLY HAVE ONE. I'VE GOT ONE QUESTION, YOU'VE GOT ONE CHANCE TO ANSWER.

I wish I could hear them --

WHO ARE YOU WORKING WITH? FALCONE OR HER?

81

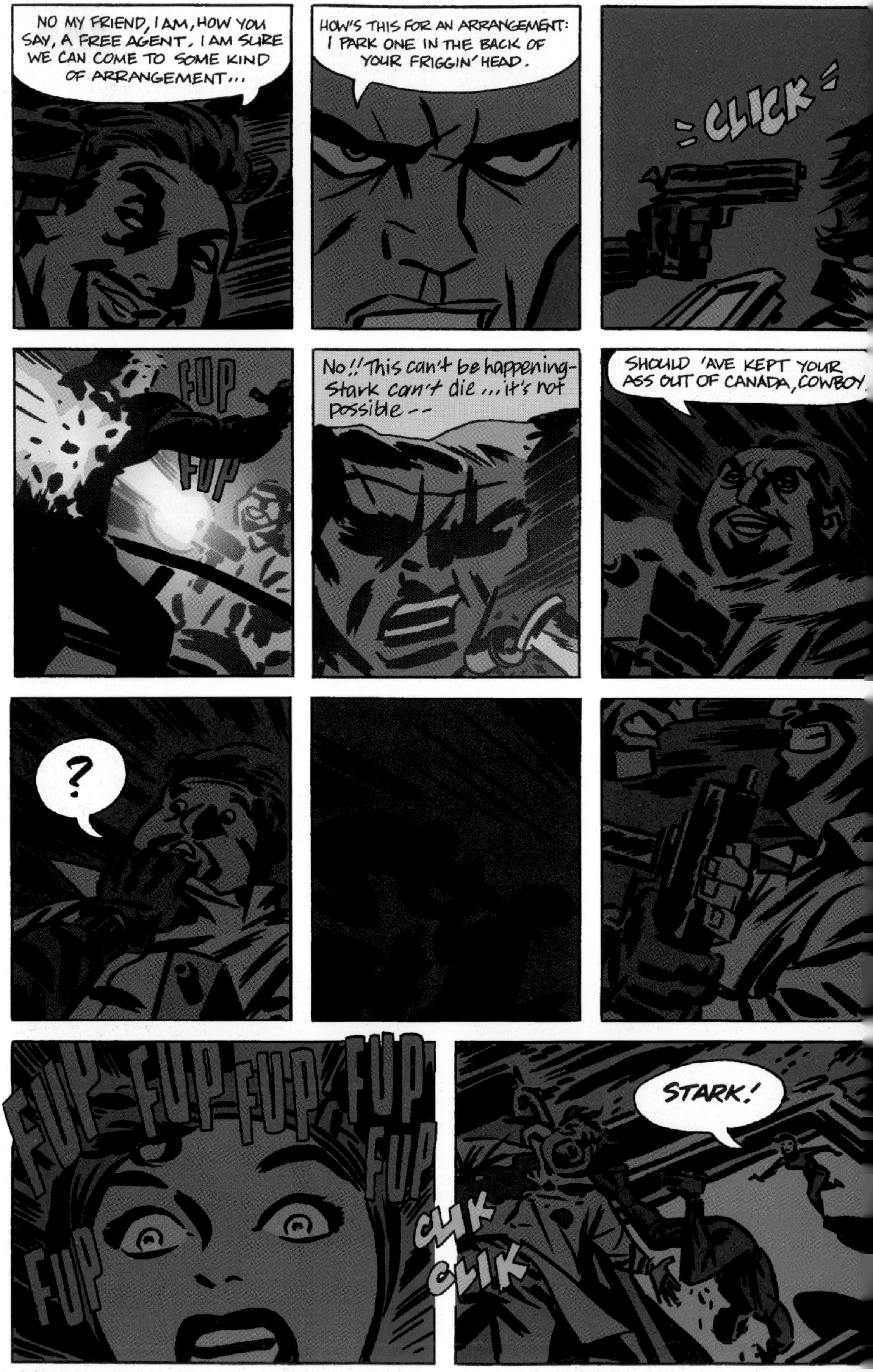
NO MY FRIEND, I AM, HOW YOU SAY, A FREE AGENT. I AM SURE WE CAN COME TO SOME KIND OF ARRANGEMENT...
HOW'S THIS FOR AN ARRANGEMENT: I PARK ONE IN THE BACK OF YOUR FRIGGIN' HEAD.
CLICK
FUP
FUP
No!! This can't be happening-Stark can't die ... it's not possible --
SHOULD 'AVE KEPT YOUR ASS OUT OF CANADA, COWBOY.
?
FUP FUP FUP FUP FUP FUP
CLIK CLIK
STARK!

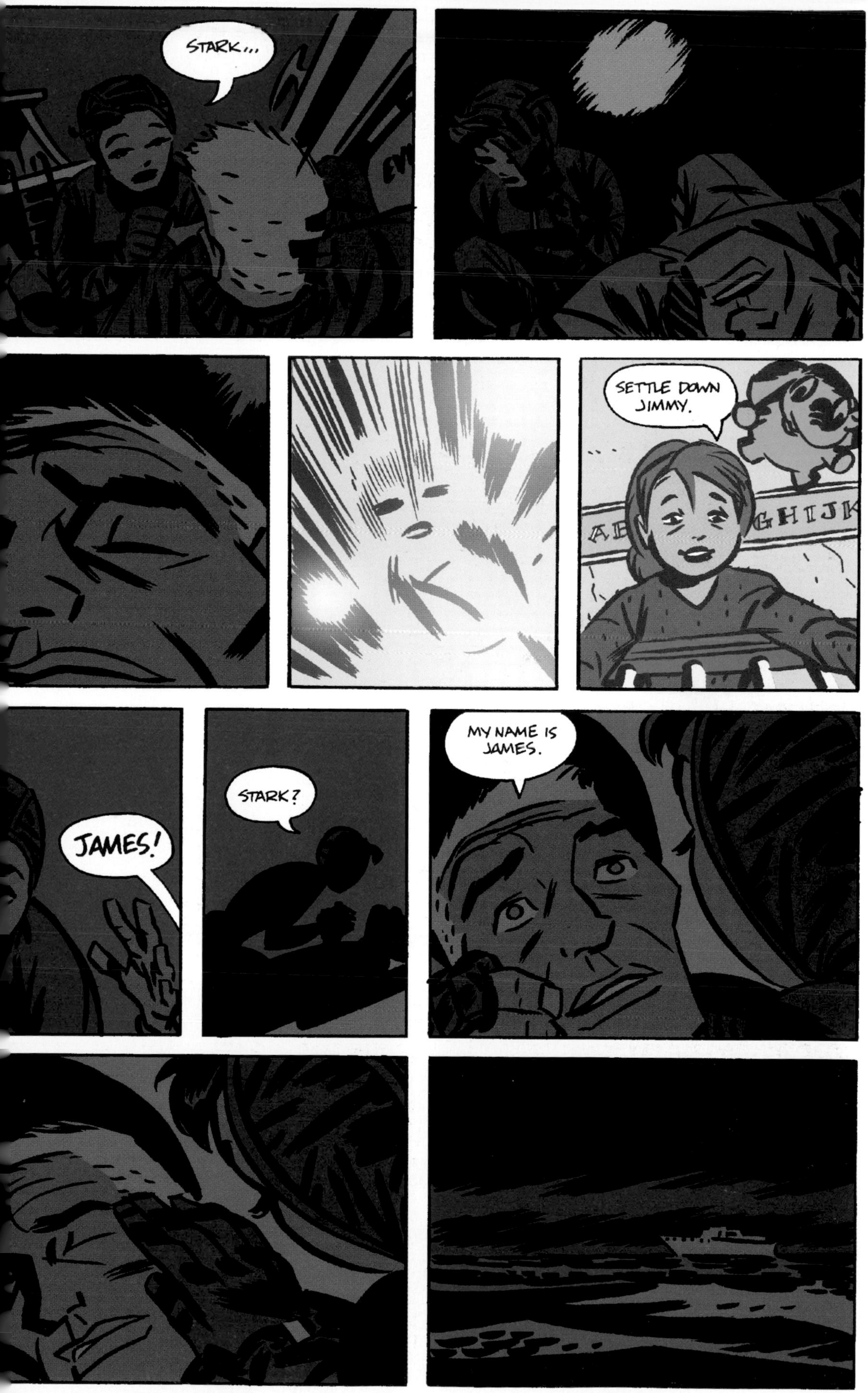
STARK...
SETTLE DOWN JIMMY.
JAMES!
STARK?
MY NAME IS JAMES.

My instincts tell me to get as far away from here as fast as possible. But I have to check the cove. If I want to stay 'dead,' I better make sure there are no loose ends.

I can feel a tidal wave of remorse inside me. I choke it back, and wade into shore.

THERE'S NO ONE HERE BUT US, SELINA.

SLAM? SLAM BRADLEY?

CHANTEL'S DEAD SELINA.

CHANTEL? DEAD? HOW--

THERE'S NO TIME FOR THAT. WHERE ARE THE OTHERS?

OTHERS? THERE ARE NO OTHERS.... ALL THE BAD MEN ARE DEAD SHERIFF....

EASY SELINA - PULL YOURSELF TOGETHER. WHAT ABOUT STARK?

GONE.

WHAT NOW, SELINA?

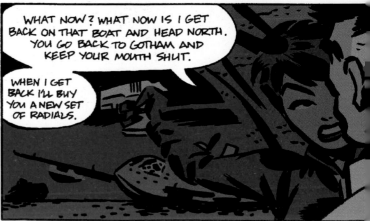

WHAT NOW? WHAT NOW IS I GET BACK ON THAT BOAT AND HEAD NORTH. YOU GO BACK TO GOTHAM AND KEEP YOUR MOUTH SHUT.

WHEN I GET BACK I'LL BUY YOU A NEW SET OF RADIALS.

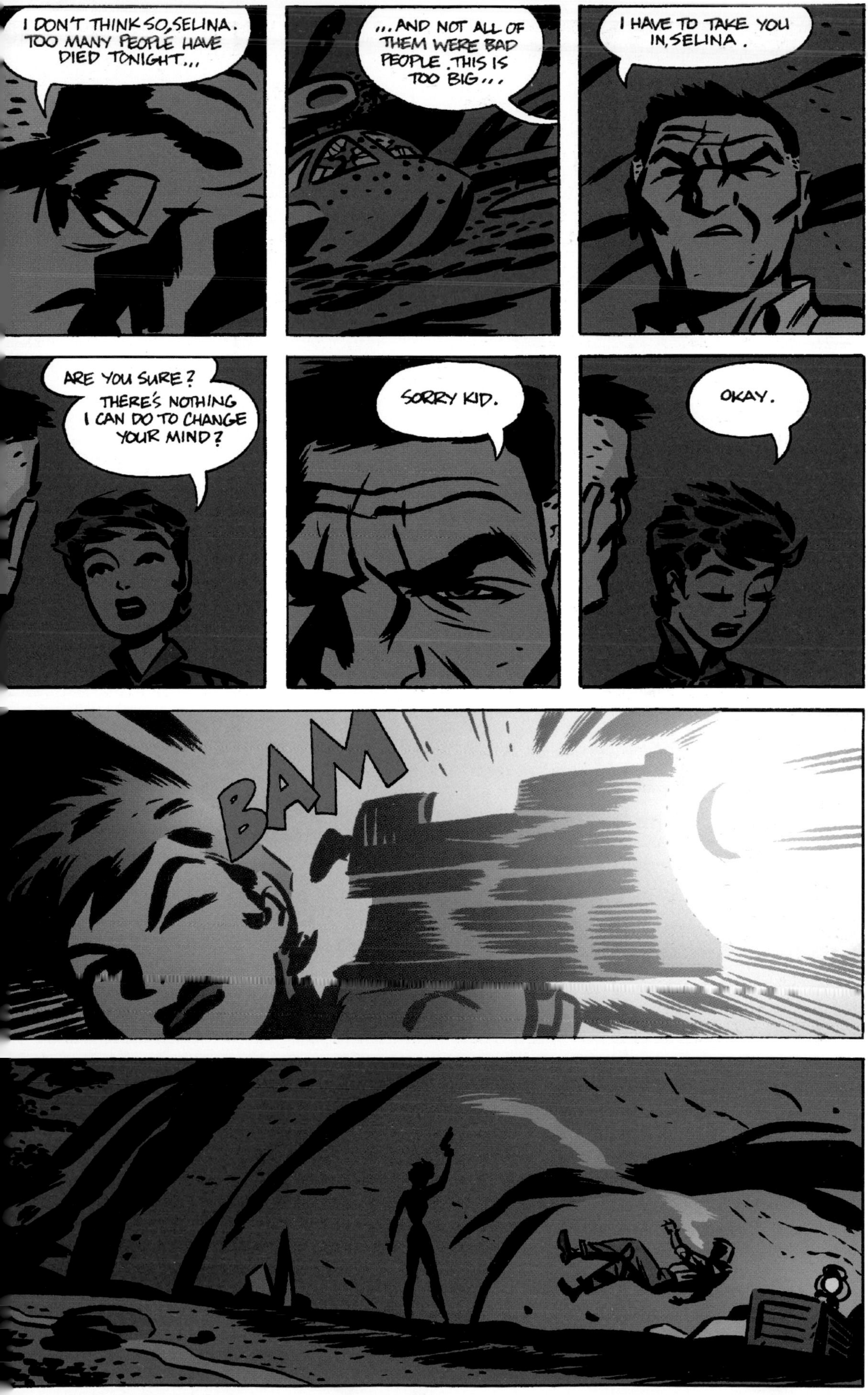
I DON'T THINK SO, SELINA. TOO MANY PEOPLE HAVE DIED TONIGHT...
...AND NOT ALL OF THEM WERE BAD PEOPLE. THIS IS TOO BIG...
I HAVE TO TAKE YOU IN, SELINA.
ARE YOU SURE? THERE'S NOTHING I CAN DO TO CHANGE YOUR MIND?
SORRY KID.
OKAY.
BAM

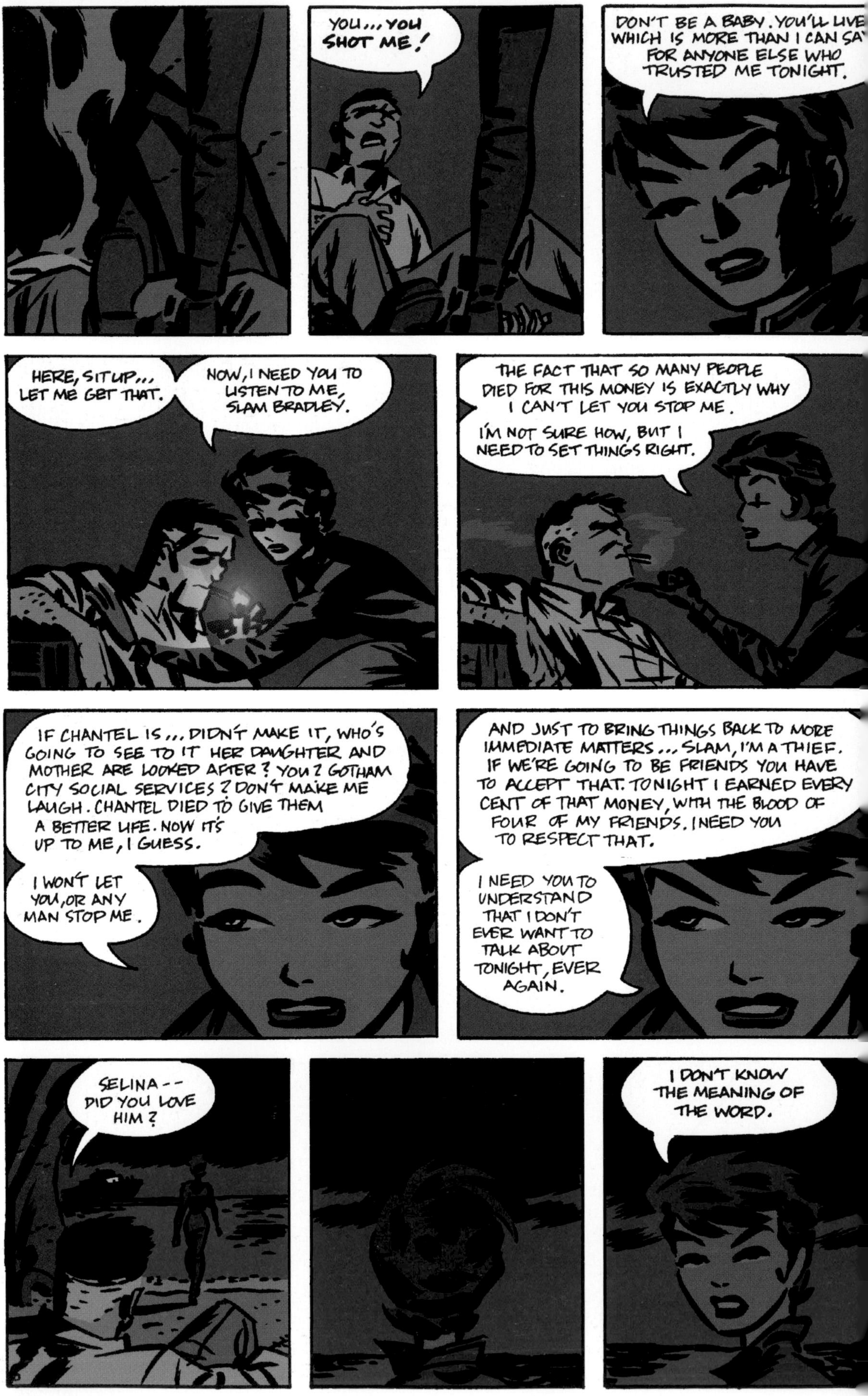

YOU... YOU SHOT ME!
DON'T BE A BABY. YOU'LL LIVE WHICH IS MORE THAN I CAN SAY FOR ANYONE ELSE WHO TRUSTED ME TONIGHT.
HERE, SIT UP... LET ME GET THAT.
NOW, I NEED YOU TO LISTEN TO ME, SLAM BRADLEY.
THE FACT THAT SO MANY PEOPLE DIED FOR THIS MONEY IS EXACTLY WHY I CAN'T LET YOU STOP ME.
I'M NOT SURE HOW, BUT I NEED TO SET THINGS RIGHT.
IF CHANTEL IS... DIDN'T MAKE IT, WHO'S GOING TO SEE TO IT HER DAUGHTER AND MOTHER ARE LOOKED AFTER? YOU? GOTHAM CITY SOCIAL SERVICES? DON'T MAKE ME LAUGH. CHANTEL DIED TO GIVE THEM A BETTER LIFE. NOW IT'S UP TO ME, I GUESS.
I WON'T LET YOU, OR ANY MAN STOP ME.
AND JUST TO BRING THINGS BACK TO MORE IMMEDIATE MATTERS... SLAM, I'M A THIEF. IF WE'RE GOING TO BE FRIENDS YOU HAVE TO ACCEPT THAT. TONIGHT I EARNED EVERY CENT OF THAT MONEY, WITH THE BLOOD OF FOUR OF MY FRIENDS. I NEED YOU TO RESPECT THAT.
I NEED YOU TO UNDERSTAND THAT I DON'T EVER WANT TO TALK ABOUT TONIGHT, EVER AGAIN.
SELINA -- DID YOU LOVE HIM?
I DON'T KNOW THE MEANING OF THE WORD.

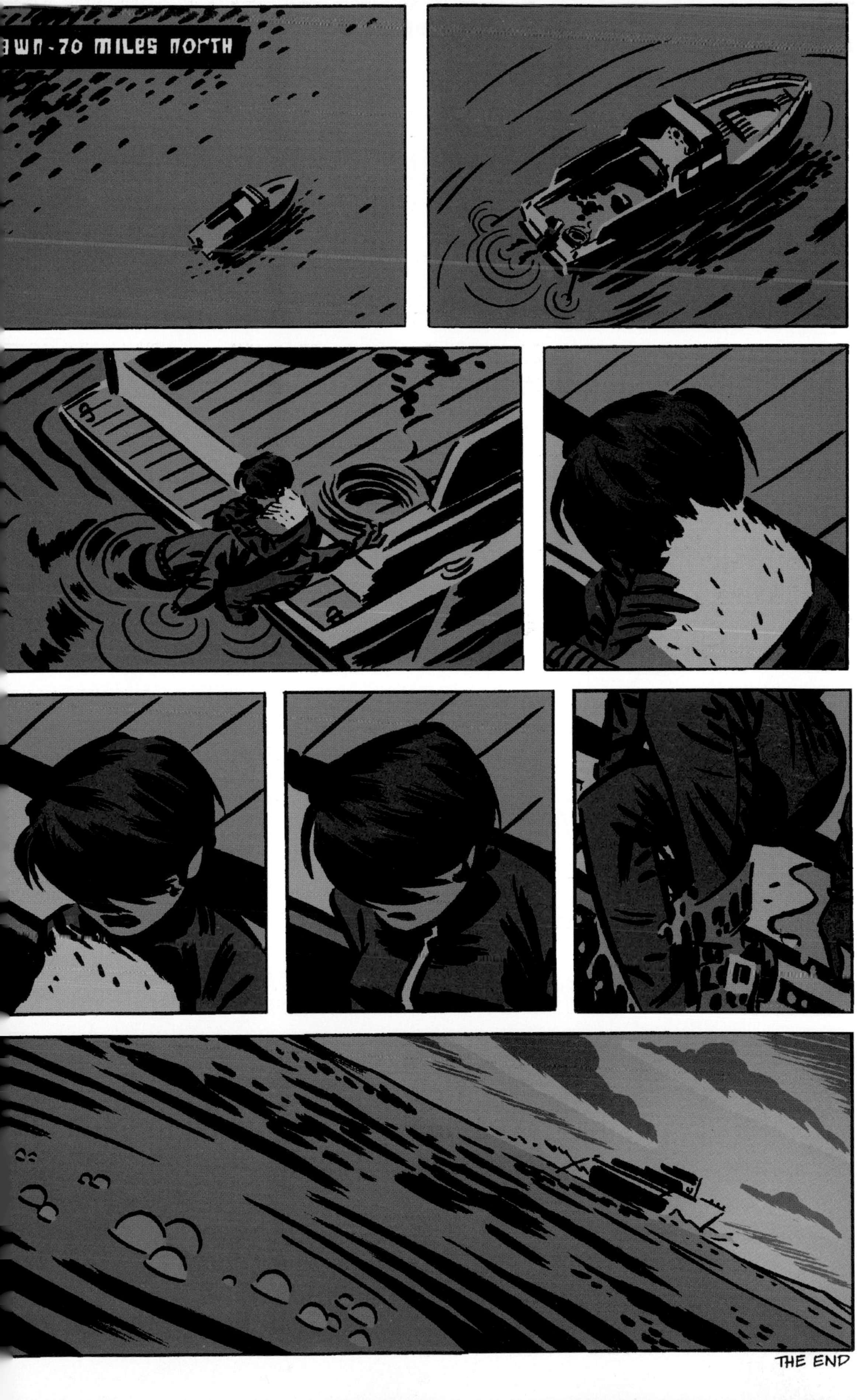

WN - 70 MILES NORTH
THE END

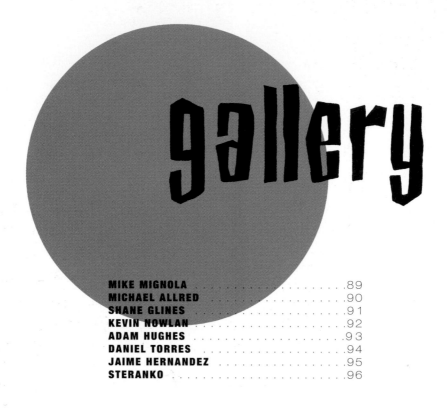

gallery

Selina's Big Score was an idea that occured to me during the development of the ongoing Catwoman series. It seemed like the perfect story for both myself and Selina to get together over. The only problem was I'd built a story that pre-dated my redesign of Catwoman's new look.

The solution is spread out before you. If I couldn't draw the new Catwoman, why not get some of the biggest talents in the business to draw her? At the risk of uncharacteristic humility, I am still stunned that the likes of these talents would take the time to grace these pages.So to Mike, Mike, Shane, Kevin, Jaime, Adam, Mr. Torres and Steranko; my heartfelt thanks.

I'd also like to take a second here to thank Ed Brubaker, my partner in crime on the Catwoman monthly, and Matt Hollingsworth, God's own colorist.

Love to all,
Darwyn
Toronto,2002

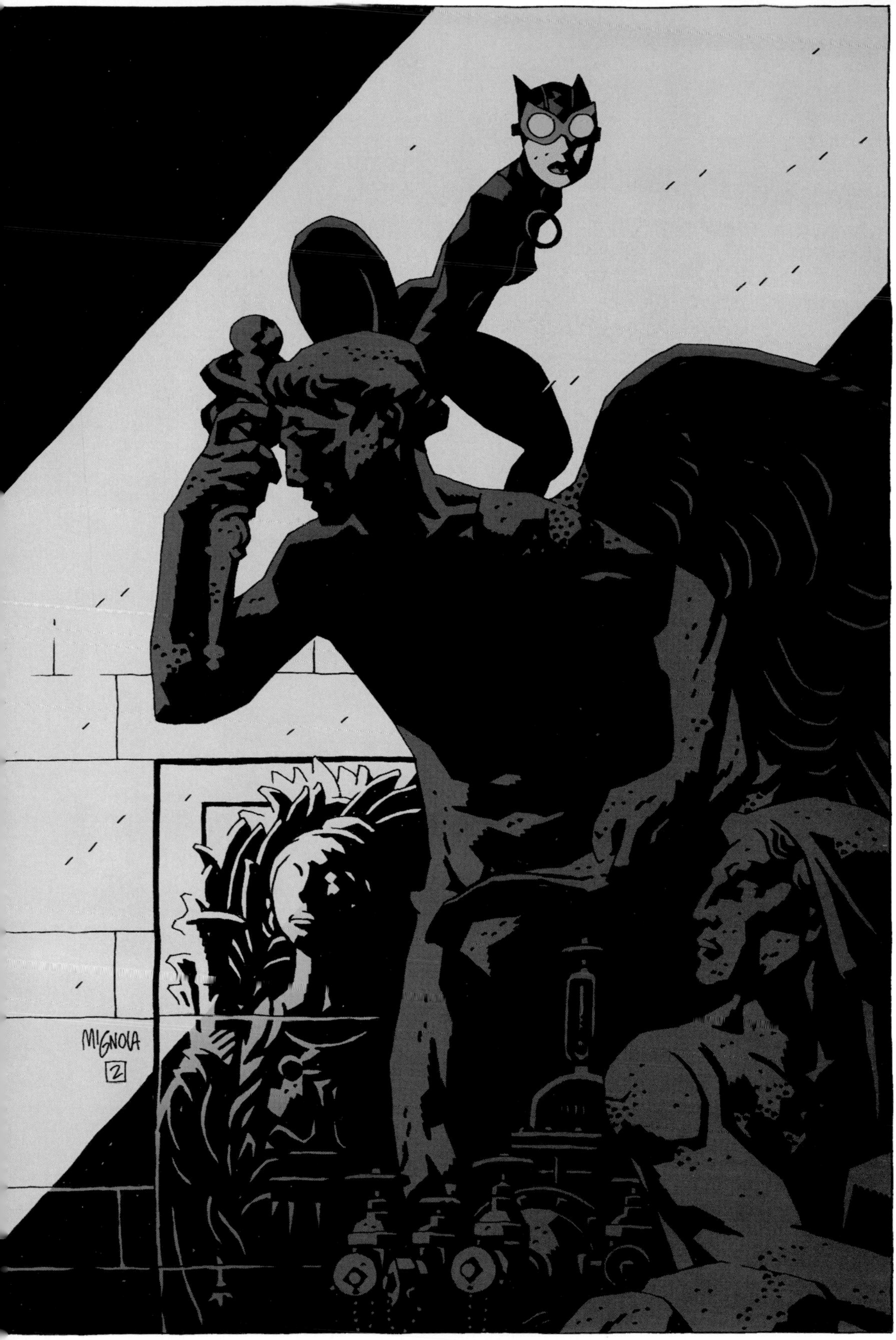
MIGNOLA
2

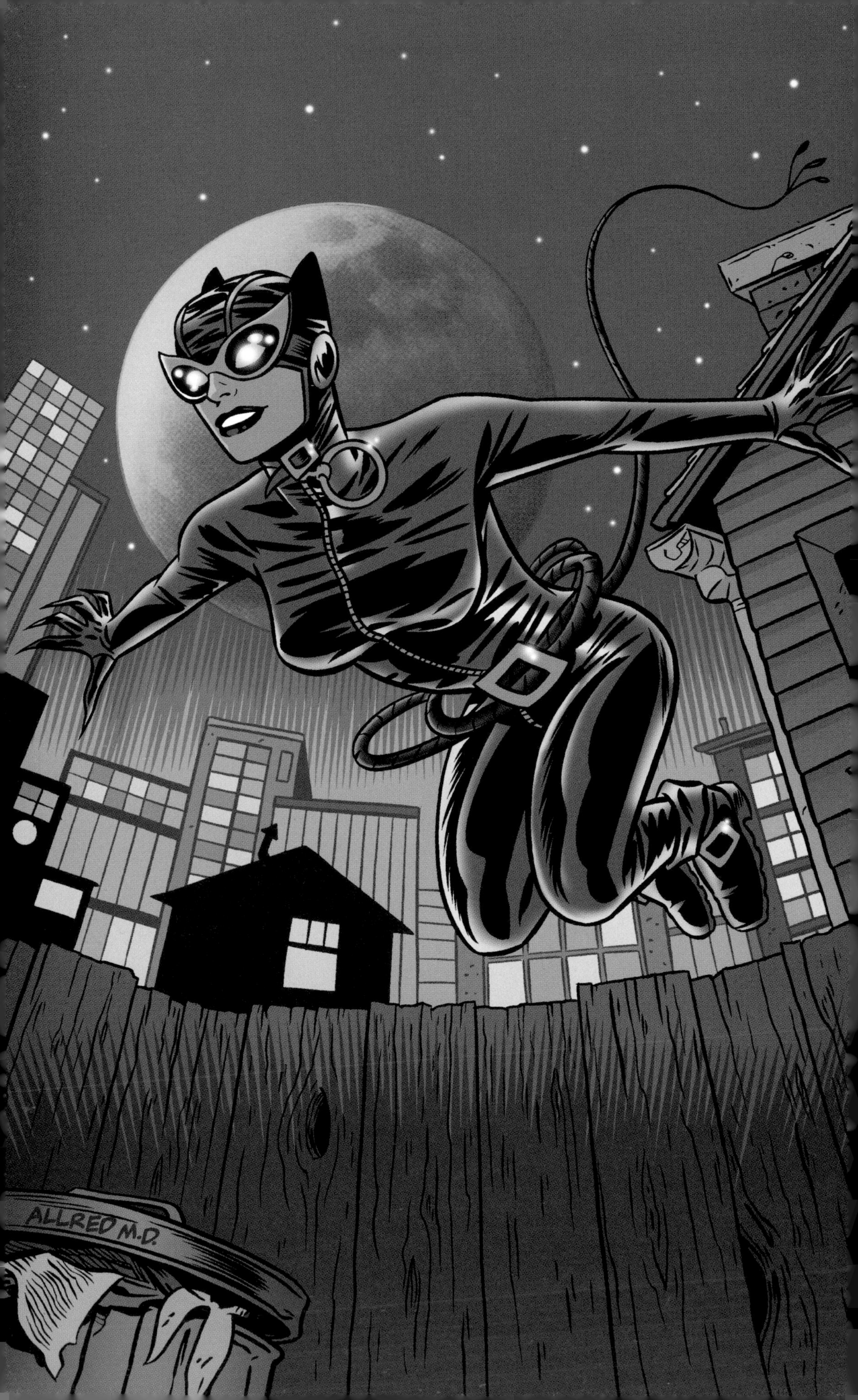
ALLRED M.D.

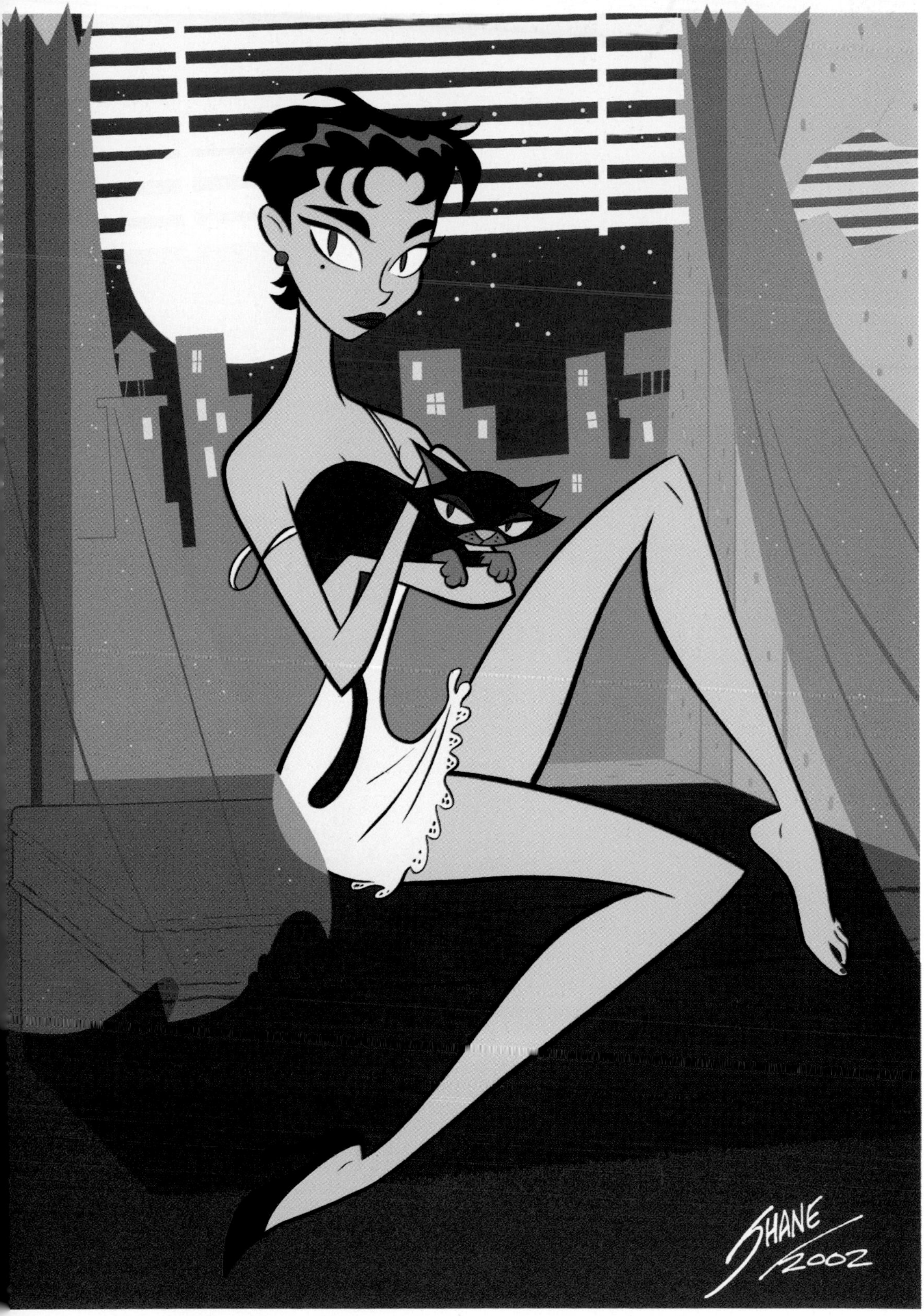
SHANE
2002

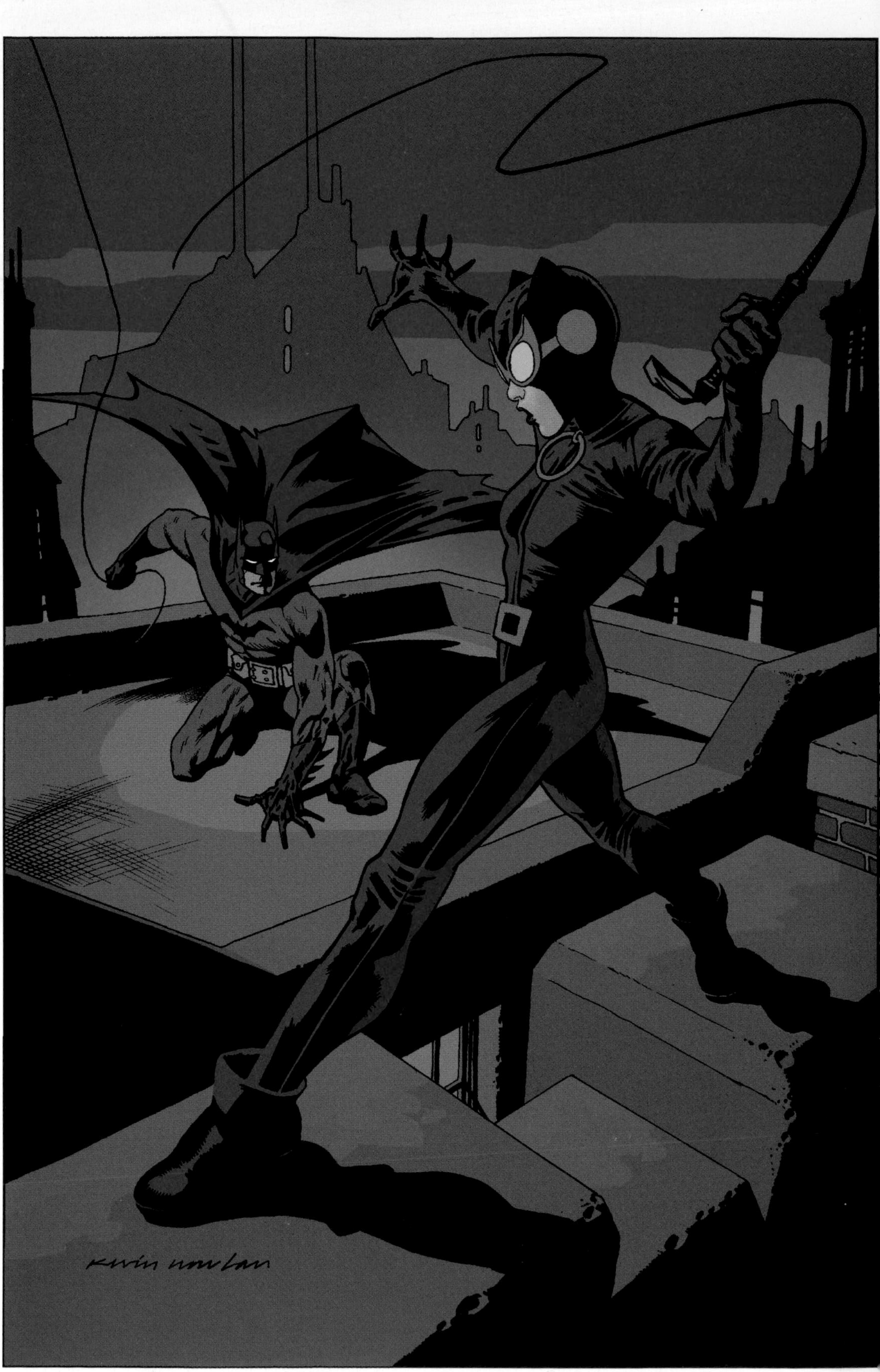
kevin nowlan

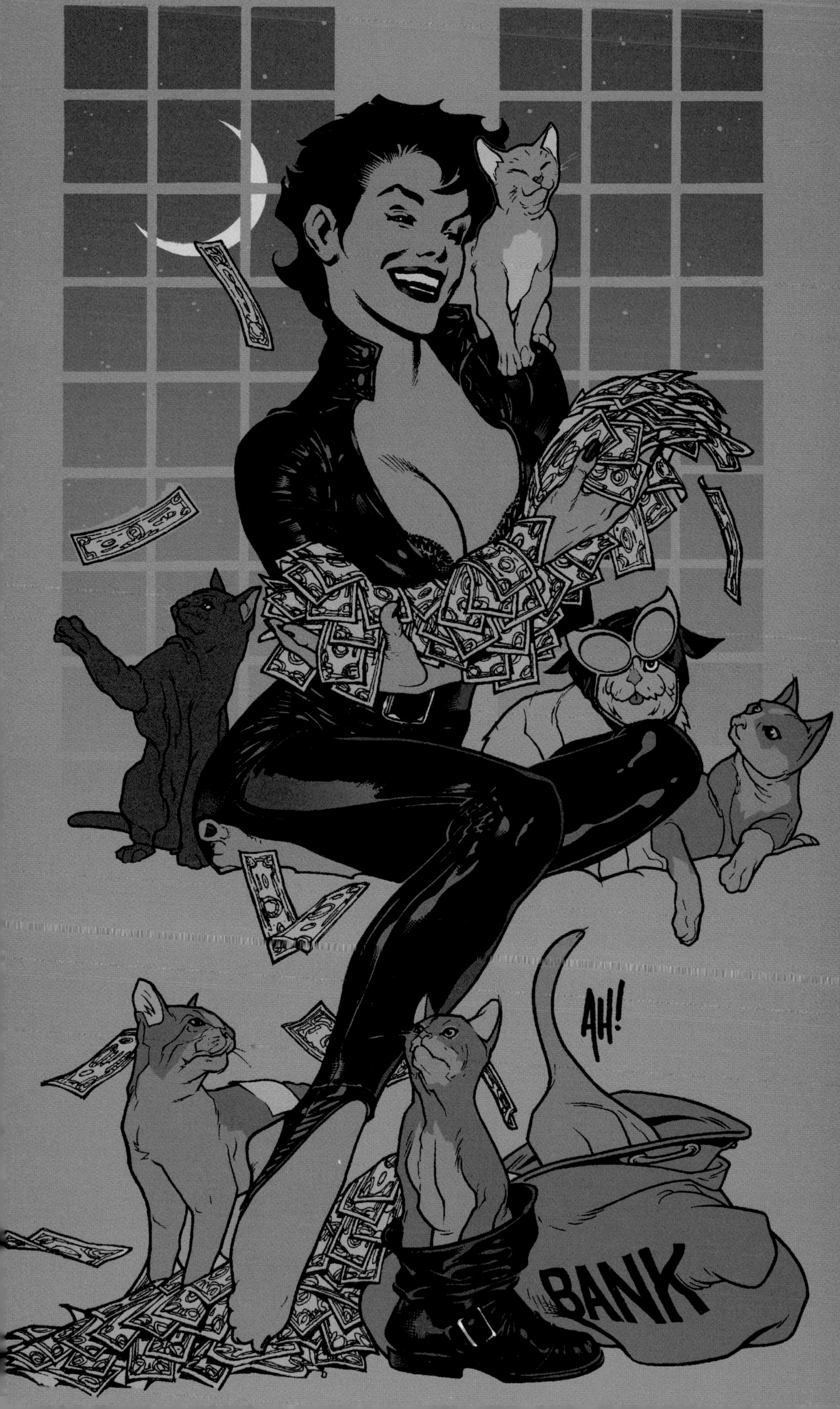
AH!
BANK

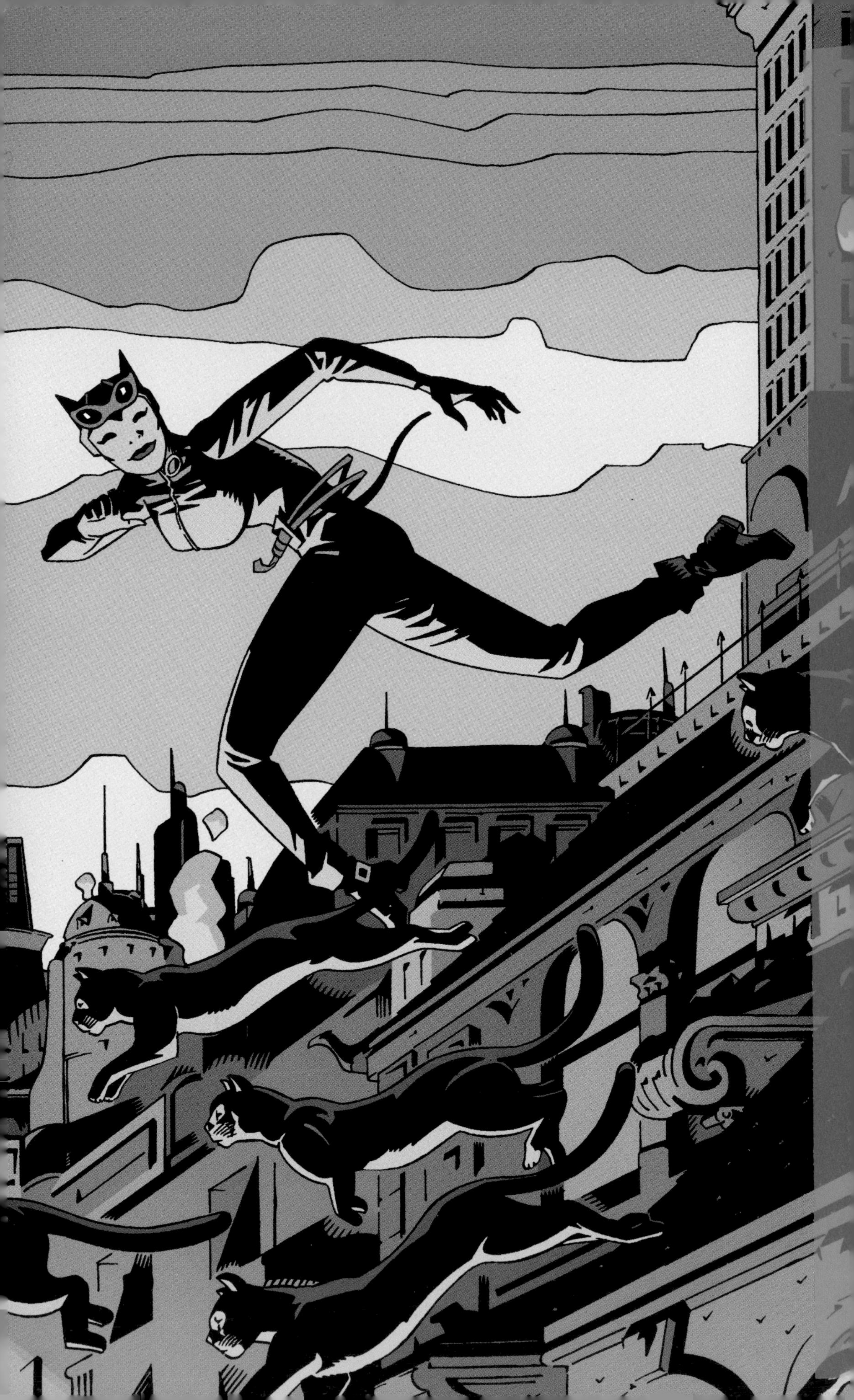

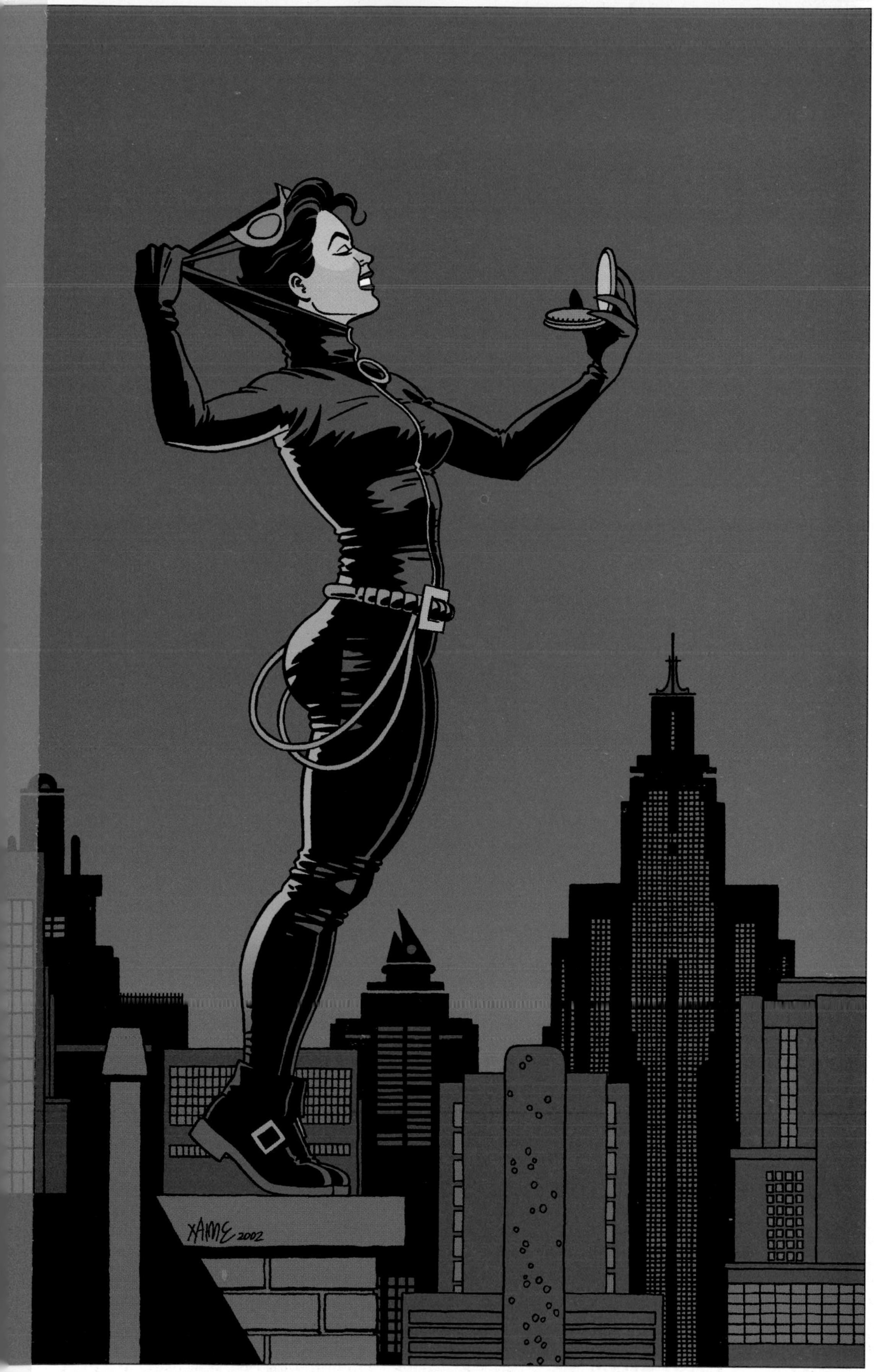
XAIME 2002

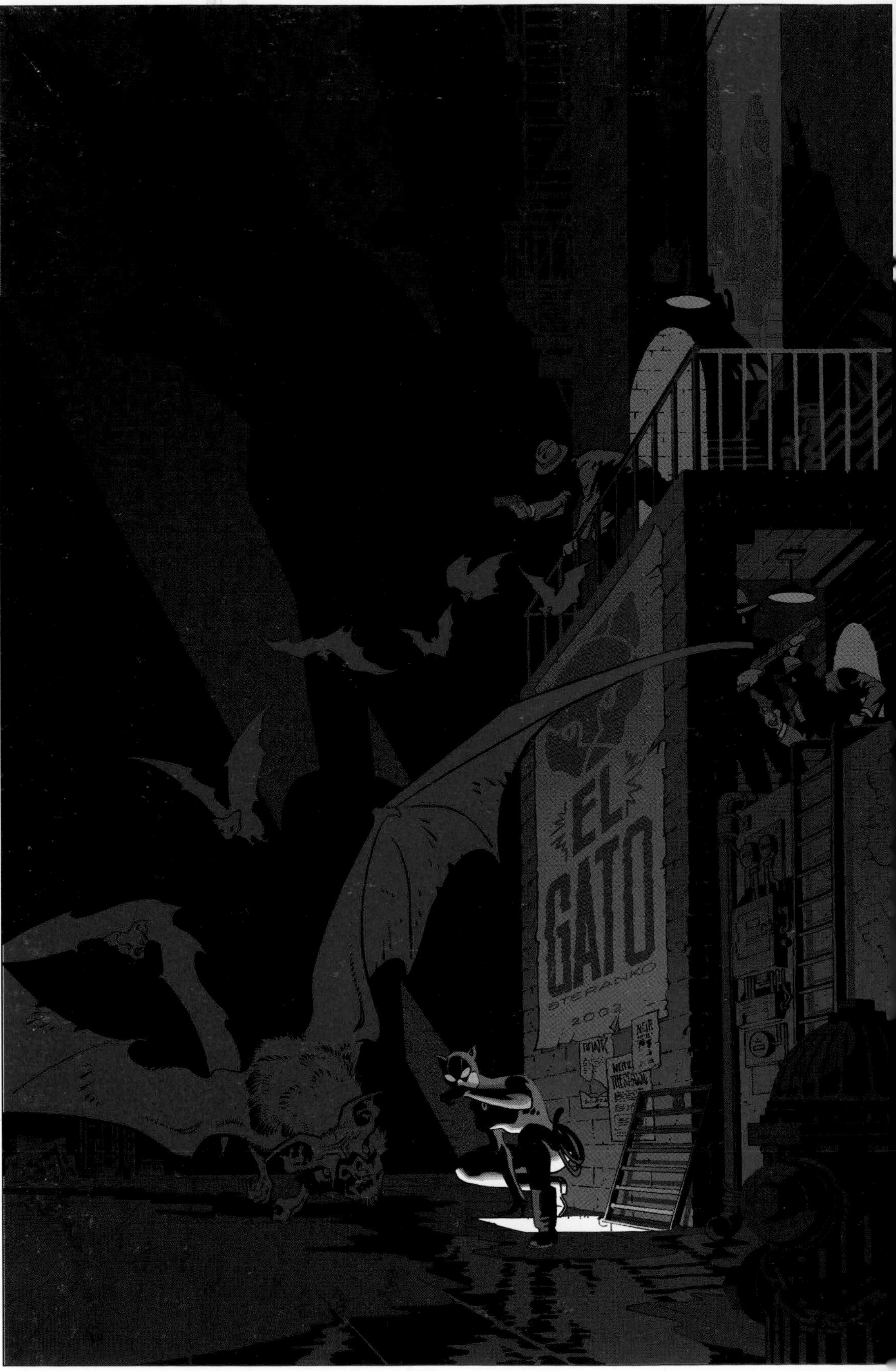
EL
GATO
STERANKO
2002